FUNDAMENTAL ACTING

A PRACTICAL GUIDE

THE APPLAUSE ACTING SERIES

ACTING IN FILM by Michael Caine

ACTING IN RESTORATION COMEDY
by Simon Callow

ACTING WITH SHAKESPEARE: The Comedies
by Janet Suzman

ACTING: Basic Technique and Variations by Paul Kuritz

THE ACTOR'S EYE: Seeing and Being Seen
by David Downs

THE ACTOR AND THE TEXT by Cicely Berry

ACCIDENTALLY ON PURPOSE by John Strasberg

THE CRAFTSMEN OF DIONYSUS by Jerome Rockwood

CREATING A CHARACTER by Moni Yakim

DIRECTING THE ACTION by Charles Marowitz

DUO! The Best Scenes for the 90s

THE MONOLOGUE WORKSHOP by Jack Poggi

ONE ON ONE: Best Monologues for the 90s (Men)

ONE ON ONE: Best Monologues for the 90s (Women)

ON SINGING ONSTAGE by David Craig

A PERFORMER PREPARES by David Craig

SHAKESCENES: Shakespeare for Two
Edited by John Russell Brown

SLINGS AND ARROWS by Bobby Lewis

SOLILOQUY! The Shakespeare Monologues (Men)

SOLILOQUY! The Shakespeare Monologues (Women)

SOLO! The Best Monologues of the 80s (Men)

SOLO! The Best Monologues of the 80s (Women)

SPEAK WITH DISTINCTION by Edith Skinner
Edited by Lilene Mansell and Timothy Monich
90-minute audiotape also available

STANISLAVSKI REVEALED by Sonia Moore

STYLE: Acting in High Comedy by Maria Aitken

THE VOCAL VISION
edited by Marian Hampton and Barbara Acker

PAUL KURITZ

FUNDAMENTAL ACTING

A PRACTICAL GUIDE

NEW YORK • LONDON

AN APPLAUSE ORIGINAL
Fundamental Acting: A Practical Guide
© 1998 by Paul Kuritz
ISBN 1-55783-304-4

Library of Congress Cataloging-in-Publication Data:

Kuritz, Paul.
    Fundamental acting : a practical guide / Paul Kuritz.
        p.   cm.
    ISBN 1-55783-304-4
    1. Acting.   I. Title
PN2061.K7868   1997
792'.028--dc21   97-27053
                                                                  CIP

British Library Cataloging-in-Publication Data:

A catalogue record for this book is available from the British Library

Applause Theatre Books
211 West 71st Street
New York, NY 10023
(212) 496-7511
FAX (212) 721-2856

Contents

Action.....Relaxation.....Objective.....Spontaneity and
Wildness.....Emotion.....Monologues.....Texts.....Projection and
Presence....Substitution.....Referential Movement....Character
Analysis.....Heightened Diction.....The Score....A Rehearsal Strategy

The Rationale.....Poetry and Verse.....Scansion.....Accent and
Rhythm.....Analyzing the Verse.....Variety.....Figures and Tropes.....
Imagery.....Speaking Verse.....Verse Dialogue.....Poetic Character

The Nature of Humor.....Incongruity and
Ignorance.....Upholding "The Normal".....Comic Power
Playing.....Superiority and Comedy.....Situation Comedy.....One
Thing at a Time.....The Vaudeville Take.....Energy, Emotion, and
Subtext.....Comic Traits.....Comic Invention.....Comic Diction.....
Comedy and Clarity.....Comic Analysis

PREFACE

You cannot learn an art from a book. You cannot teach an art from a book. So if those were your reasons for picking this book up, read no further. There are other books which claim to do both of these things.

If you want to learn to act, find an actor or director whose own work you like and ask that person to teach you. Acting is learned from a living artist not a book page.

If you are to teach acting, rather than immediately look for a book, think about what you would like your students to know how to do. Then think about why you would like the young actors to learn these things. After you have organized your own thoughts, gather your students and ask them to do things on stage. React to what they do, seeking to help them learn the things you thought about. Trust that your experience and judgement will see you through.

"Why then have you written a book about acting?", you may rightly ask. This book organizes my own thoughts about what I have asked student actors to know and to do. This book may turn the monologue in your head about acting into a dialogue. Maybe there are things in this book which you will want to try; maybe there are things you think are foolish. Take and use what is helpful. Acting stays fresh when its teachers are alert to borrowing on behalf of their students.

I have found that typical beginning acting students want three things. First, they want a technique which allows them to effectively play serious realistic dramas. Second, they want to be able to handle a comic role. And third, they want advice on how to begin to approach Shakespearean verse.

This book is designed with the beginning acting students' desires in mind. The book begins by bringing students in front of an audience, as themselves, to perform everyday activities. Gradually, other tasks — pursuing an objective, encountering an obstacle, actively listening, responding to inner stimuli, generating an emotion, speaking a memorized text, substituting personal images, playing a character, etc — are introduced to the simple everyday activity. As a result of these cumulative exercises, students learn a basic technique for performing a realistic character.

Building upon the realistic technique, the next two parts of the book introduce acting students to the two most challenging aspects of acting — playing comedy and speaking verse. As with the first part, the techniques are introduced gradually through a series of simple exercises. In fact, the purpose if this text is to keep the reading brief and the doing long. Most acting texts hold more than a teacher wants or needs for an individual course. This book is brief and easily adapted to at least three acting courses, such as beginning acting, acting comedy, and classical acting.

The book is appropriate for all beginning actors, whether in junior colleges,

colleges, universities, and performance conservatories. Some students like the comfort of having a text to which they can refer. Throughout this text, what actors do on stage is measured by the logic of everyday life. While this is common in teaching realistic acting, the text may be singular in presenting verse and comedy in this light. Indeed, the text may be unique in the emphasis comic performance receives. I believe this book presents the most thorough analysis of an actor's work in comedy available.

Many people have helped with this book: my students and colleagues at Bates College; the president and dean of the college who have supported both my travel and research; the Theatre faculty and students of Bratislava, Slovakia's Academy of the Arts, especially Vladimir Strnisko; and, of course, my family — Deborah, Nathaniel, Ethan, James, and Stefan, whose lives simultaneously challenged and supported my ideas before they were ever tested in the classroom: this book is for them.

INTRODUCTION

by Howard Stein

Former Dean of Faculty and Students, Yale School of Drama

This textbook on acting is an unconventional text. It is humble, it is more of a guidebook than a how — to book, it respects the reader as a human being as well as a student (or teacher) of acting, and it concentrates on two areas (seldom if ever) discussed in a book on the subject of performing: poetry and comedy. The reader is in for a special treat and an especially valuable experience.

Kuritz is an imaginiative teacher who knows that acting has to be caught as much as it has to be taught. Most teachers of acting, despite their haste to respect the craft of acting, feel convinced of the teachability of acting. Kuritz does not minimize the teaching aspect by which one develops the craft of acting; what he adds, however, is the recognition that the student of acting must position herself or himself to catch acting secrets and techniques, must prepare herself or himself with the human awareness that must be brought to the scene in order to catch the proper method of being believable. Kuritz provides the reader with fertile ground, not just because he offers exercises, but because he offers attitudes, thoughts, examples, information, all those qualities which provide fertile ground in which a plant can gain sustenance for growth. The reader is the plant, and Kuritz provides the soil, the sun, and leads the reader to the water necessary for flowering. This book is a rare privilege.

The second portion of the book is given over to poetry, that form in which the theater had its beginnings. Aristotle's book on the drama (theater) is titled, "The Poetics." Rather than find poetry foreign to the drama, Kuritz like Aristotle, finds it central to the drama and to the theater. He also finds it central to the human spirit. Most students and teachers are frightened by the presence of poetry, annoyed by its difficulty, and hostile to its mystery. Kuritz dispells all these myths, and because he knows the value of poetry to each and every reader, makes the language and dynamics of poetry easily accessible to the reader. Rather than indulge the terror most often felt by theatrical people to confront poetry, Kuritz welcomes the advent of the poet and submerges himself in the poet's genius. He therefore provides for the student of theater a rare, rare gift, the engagement of a young, naive, stage struck perhaps, eager, inspired, ambitious, student or teacher the opportunity to revel in the beauties and values of poetry. Shakespearee is not a foreign language to Kuritz and will not be a foreign language to his reader. The beauty, the clarity, the profundity of the poet suddenly becomes immediately available to his reader. Every young person knows how meaningful beautiful language is if no other reason than the absence of beautiful language in her or his everyday life. We are buried in pedestrian speech, and yearn for beauty in our conversations. Kuritz doesn't try to educate us; he simply exposes us to the intricacies and again to the value of poetry in the theater, providing the reader with the confidence and the comfort to express the poet's words. An acting student (or teacher) is given, then, a dimension almost always lacking in acting instruction in this country. Just as poetry is natural for the youngest human being (nursery rhymes are not by chance!), so poetry is natural for the theater artist. Bravo Mr Kuritz.

Now for comedy. The reader of this book is living at a time when comedy is even more significant than it has been in the past. I recently wrote a chapter in a book, a chapter called, "Do We have To Be Funnier Than We Used To have To Be?" with the answer given in no uncertain terms, "Yes! You Bet!" I don't try to explain that conclusion, but I do make it without any reservation. Look at the contemporary plays and see the role of comedy: *As Is* (the first major play about AIDS which has a laugh track all the way through!), *End Of The World With Symposium to Follow*, Kopit's play which has as its subject the title itself and is filled with raucuous laughter, even Arthur Miller's *Broken Glass* during which people kept turning to each other saying, "I never knew Arthur Miller was so funny." The writers frequently writing out of a poetic spirit are writing plays filled with irony, paradox, ambiguity, and satire. To perform the contemporary playwrights, actors need not only a sense of humor onto an audience, BECAUSE THE PLAYWRIGHT HAS MADE SUCH PROJECTION AN IMPERATIVE. Any student needs to know comedy, its secrets, its difficulties, and its execution. No longer can the actor rely on authenticity alone to perform in today's theater. An actor may not be witty, but today's actor has to know wit when she or he hears it, *enjoy* wit, treasure wit, and if possible love wit. Comedy has become the single serious expression during the last few decades and will continue uninterrupted, I am sure, for the next century. We have discovered the riches, the profundity, and the pleasure of comedy. Varieties of comedy are endless, unlike tragedies. The acting student and teacher must be informed of those varieties, must seek them out, and must project them to make them accessible. Acting comedy, as Kuritz makes clear, is the most difficult kind of acting to master. It is also the most satisfying, the most complex, and in the end the most valuable. Kuritz equips his reader with the most significant elements for genuine success in the craft of acting. I know no other text which takes comedy so seriously. My congratulations, my admiration, and my gratitude to him.

BASIC TECHNIQUE

"Probably a good actor is one who hasn't grown up yet."[1]

—Dennis Hopper

Many actors share Dennis Hopper's opinion. "I remember Marlon Brando gave an interview years ago. He said he wanted to give up acting because he wanted to finally grow up. And everybody said, 'Oh, that's terrible.' At the time, I defended that because I understood it. It's hard work to stay a child and have a child-like feeling, imagination."

It was even hard for that eternal child, Peter Pan. Once he had defeated Captain Hook, Peter, according to Barrie's stage directions, became "a very Napoleon on his ship...in Hook's hat and cigars, and with a small iron claw."[2] Every Peter—every youthful life force—grows a Hook—a sense of inevitable mortality. Actors fight growing up. For them, every performance is a new beginning.

ACTION

As far as we know, human beings are unique among living things in the realization of their own mortality. Human beings alone know they will die. Art arises from human beings' need to confront the knowledge of personal death. Faced with the knowledge of our own end, we seek to understand why we are here, and what we can do until the end comes. This knowledge produces another distinctive trait—storytelling.

So awesome and profound are the facts of our human situation, that we need to tell each other about how we have, and will, confront the time available to us. Storyteller Isak Dinesen (1885–1962) supposedly said that anything can be tolerated if you can turn it into a story. Most of our days are filled with stories, either of what we have done, heard, or seen, or of what we hope, fear, or plan to do. Even when we sleep, we tell ourselves stories with dreams. And when we die, all that remains are the stories people will tell of us. Art expresses our insights into the nature of life, death, and human existence in a variety of imaginative ways. Past and future events meet in the present act of storytelling, one of the oldest arts, and a grandparent of the dramatic theater.

With the dramatic theater, storytelling became direct enactment. Instead of telling what actions other people did, storytellers did the actions themselves, and, in the process, became actors. On the theater's stage, people stand before other people and do other people's actions **AS IF** they were their own. The actions may derive from history, from fantasy, or from a mixture of both. So wondrous can the event be, that the Russian acting teacher Constantin Stanislavski (1863–1938) called it "magic."

The dramatic theater is the art of total action. In music, experiences are conveyed through sound; music exists only in time. In sculpture, expression is limited to a fixed, three-dimensionality; sculpture exists only in space. The people on the dramatic theater's stage — actors — do all kinds of actions. Like dance, the dramatic theater's other grandparent, the dramatic theater is a time and space art.

The actor's own mind, body, and voice constitute the actor's instrument. In music and painting, the artist and the material are easily distinguished. One artist can play another's violin or use another artist's brush, for example. However, an actor cannot borrow another actor's instrument. Consequently, actors can only play themselves.

Does this mean that an actor will be the same in every part? It can. Some actors have made successful careers by revealing their strong personalities in a variety of roles. Other actors have seemed to assume a distinct personality for each role. The difference between a great and a good actor comes down to the depth of the actor's mind, the range of the actor's voice, and the flexibility of the actor's body. If the actor's instrument were a piano, great actors would have instruments with many and various keys, while personality actors would have instruments with a few, but compelling, keys.

Everyone has thought, spoken, and moved; so everyone has experience acting. And everyone has done believable and truthful actions. An actor is an artist who does actions — mental, verbal, and physical actions — in front of other people. An actor does not pretend to do actions, any more than we pretend to do actions in everyday life, or any more than a pianist pretends to hit the keys. *Indeed, the logic of life is the actor's first guide to truthful and believable actions on stage.* Why, then, can't everyone act on stage?

The great Russian acting teacher, Constantin Stanislavski, noticed that people change when then get in front of a group of people. They may feel self-conscious. They may tense up. They may feel obliged to entertain the audience. Some people are paralyzed, while others fly into wild exaggeration. Still other people do something they think is acting: they enlarge actions or indicate emotions. Some people imitate the behavior of others in an attempt to prove to the audience their understanding of what is expected of them. Stanislavski believed that actor training should begin by helping people do in public what they normally only do in private.

RELAXATION

Most people believe that their private lives are neither very interesting nor worthy of an audience's attention. This belief can produce anxiety and tension in people asked to repeat those actions in public. A first step in actor training should be to realize what the American philosopher Ralph Waldo Emerson (1803–82) came to believe, that "the deeper [one] dives into [one's] privatest, secretest presentiment, to [one's] wonder, [one] finds this is the most acceptable, most public, and universally true."[3] Emerson's observation belies the common belief that actors come to the theater to hide from their true selves; in fact, actors find the theater the only place where they are free to be their true selves.

☞ 1. Get in front of your group and look at them as they look at you. Stay there for about two or three minutes. Notice how you feel. Then give yourself a goal, like learning how many people are wearing sneakers or earrings. With a goal, you should notice that your self-consciousness and tension decrease. Stanislavski concluded that actors can attain relaxation by concentrating on the accomplishment of a specific task or goal. Purposelessness causes anxiety. Purposelessness allows the mind to wander out of the present, here-and-now, either to worry about the past, or to fear the future. In the specific present, all is well, and the object of concentration, variously called the **OBJECTIVE** or **INTENTION**, keeps you in the moment.

OBJECTIVE

Nobel prize-winning author I. B. Singer (1904–91) told a story:

> "Once a boy came over to the *cheder* where I studied, and he said, 'Do you know that my father wanted to box my ears?' So the teacher said, "How do you know that he wanted to box your ears?' And the boy said, 'He did it.' A man may sit for hours and talk to you about what he thinks. But what he really is, you can judge best by what he did."[4]

Some actors love to talk about what their characters feel. They are always "working on their character". But when on stage, effective actors keep their energies focused on their **objective**. The objective is your target. Accomplish your objective, and you have hit the target.

As in life, we often pursue objectives other than the ones we say we are pursuing. Sometimes people visit psychiatrists who reveal to them the hidden objectives they were pursuing. But in both life and on the stage, actions, what we do, reveal more about what we want, than what we say. And since play texts are mostly words, actors must read carefully and employ their imaginations to invent believable and compelling character objectives.

The following words can have two very different readings, depending upon the intention:

"No please don't stop"

If the speaker wanted the other person to continue, the line could be read, "No. Please don't stop!" On the other hand, if the objective was to halt the other person's actions, then the line could be read, "No. Please don't. Stop!" Audiences come to the theatre to discover readings unimaginable to them at home.

For many actors, the objective is the most important aspect of their acting technique. Without an energizing objective, the actor is guilty of loitering.

☞ 2.   Perform a commonplace activity before your group. Use the actual objects needed to do the action. Choose a specific activity which requires some skill, or is moderately difficult, and has an element of urgency about it. Keep you attention on the actual doing of each little detail. A difficult task focuses your attention more than an easy one, and is more interesting for an audience to watch. Your goal should be to do the activity just **AS IF** you were in private. Don't pretend to do any part of the activity.

Sometimes the attainment of an objective puts you in a relationship with another person.

☞   3.   Perform your commonplace activity on stage in the company of another person performing his or her everyday activity. Acknowledge the other's presence without losing focus on your own activity. Other people should be viewed as either a potential aid, or a potential hindrance, to the accomplishment of your intention.

SPONTANEITY AND WILDNESS

One of the most important characteristics of everyday human action is **SPONTANEOUS ADAPTATION**. Theoreticians of comedy rightly point out that a machine-like inflexibility produces laughter. Even routine actions are slightly different each time we do them because we are humans and not machines. Few of our everyday actions are deliberative, labored, or preconceived; most of our actions are actually instantaneous reactions.

Socialization has made us less spontaneous and more thoughtful. To progress as actors, you need to reclaim your original "wildness." The poet Robert Bly (1926-) suggests "that every modern male has, lying at the bottom of his psyche, a large primitive being covered with hair down to his feet. Making contact with this Wild Man is the step the male has yet to take."[5] Psychologist Clarissa Pinkola Estes urges women to discover their natural wolf-like wildness to become a "Wild Woman": "Healthy wolves and healthy women share certain psychic characteristics: keen sensing, playful spirit, and a heightened capacity for devotion. Wolves and women are relational by nature, inquiring, possessed of great endurance and strength.... They are experienced in adapting to constantly changing circumstances; they are fiercely stalwart and very brave."[6] Acting requires men and women to return to their original impulses, free from the constraining thoughts of social approval or reproach.

Actors need to regain the spontaneous, reactive quality in their stage work. The great American composer John Cage (1912–92) encouraged his students with the Zen-like koan, "Don't think!—Fart!" Baseball Hall-of-Famer Yogi Berra (1925–) advises, "You can't think and hit at the same time." Like athletes, actors need to allow their emotional stream of consciousness to lead their actions. Plan your everyday activity, but go with the flow. As heavyweight boxer Mike Tyson pointed out, your game plan ends with the first punch. Respond to what is happening around you, while keeping on task. Acknowledge and adapt to changes in your circumstances, but strive to hit your target.

The paradoxical task of pursuing one's goal while adapting to changing circumstances was vividly demonstrated by basketball coach, Robert Knight. While conducting a half court drill, Coach Knight stopped the action to criticize a defensive player for not leaving his position — adapting — to pursue the ball and to prevent a basket. Play resumed, until Coach Knight stopped the action again to criticize the same player for not maintaining his position to prevent the opponent from scoring!

When the great acting teacher Sanford Meisner (1905–97) placed two actors onstage in a Repetition Exercise, the actors faced a paradoxical task, similar to the one encountered by Coach Knight's players. One actor observed something about the other actor. The other actor repeated the observation, but from his or her own perspective:

"Your shirt is red."

"My shirt is red."

The dialogue repeated, unmechanically and unplanned, until something happened to change it. The "something" had to arise spontaneously from within the actor, rather than be planned or decided beforehand. Meisner would either admonish the players: "Don't do anything until something happens to make you," or criticize them for insensitivity to the changing dynamics!

Actors repeated Meisner's exercise until "something happened":

"So what!"

"So what? I hate red!"

One of the partners instinctively sensed the effect the repetition was having and spontaneously commented on it. On other occasions, Meisner would stop the exercise if he sensed an actor was thinking about what to say before speaking. The actor, like the basketball player, has to pursue the objective — repetition — while adapting to the changing circumstances — "something happening."

After you become adept at the Repetition Exercise, you will begin to notice how much repetition exists in our everyday discourse. Plays, especially modern realistic plays, likewise contain much repetition. But the Repetition Exercise has other objectives. First, the exercise monitors your state of listening; if you can repeat, you are listening. Second, the exercise keeps your focus of attention outside of yourself, where it can be perceived both by the other actor and the audience. Third, repetition keeps your consciousness in the present here-and-now; while listening and repeating you cannot get into your mind as it thinks about what has just happened or thinks about what to do. Repetition forces your actions to spring spontaneously from an inner, emotional source, rather than from a calculated, mental source.

☞   4.   Repeat Exercise 3. This time one actor should ob-
          serve something about either the other actor or the
          other activity. Engage in Meisner's Repetition Exer-
          cise.

☞   5.   Repeat Exercise 3. This time one actor should tell a
          true or made-up story about something embarrass-
          ing that happened to her or him. Engage in Meis-

ner's Repetition Exercise. Don't go on with the story until something happens to make you.

Sometimes your objective directly involves another person. In those cases, your target is in the other actor. This allows you to directly monitor your progress by observing the other player's reactions to your efforts.

☞ 6. Invent an objective, something simple that you want the other actor either to do for you or to give to you. Repeat Exercise 3 while pursuing the chosen objective. The other actor should invent reasons, justifications, and explanations of why he or she is unable to help you.

The great Russian actor Michael Chekhov (1891–1955) noted that the actor's primary audience is the other actor on stage. For example, if John is playing Jim the Gentleman Caller in Tennessee Williams' *The Glass Menagerie* and Mary is playing Laura, the audience in the theater seats will believe that Laura loves Jim if Mary can convince John that she really does love him, that she isn't just acting! In Shakespeare's *Hamlet*, the audience will believe that Laertes wants to kill Hamlet if the actor playing Laertes can convince the actor playing Hamlet that his animosity is genuine. Good actors often fool themselves as well as their audience!

EMOTION

Emotion has been called the "sweat" of acting. In previous exercises, you may have observed or experienced some of this sweat. Emotion is the result of pursuing an objective and meeting resistance, called an **OBSTACLE**. When you pursued your objectives and met with resistance from your partner, emotion emerged. As you sought to complete your everyday activity, while your partner observed and questioned you, emotion resulted.

We respond, consciously or unconsciously, through our senses and our central nervous system, to everything we encounter in life. Following sensation, perception occurs. In this way, every action is literally a reaction. Everything is sensed and perceived as one of two possibilities: [+] good, pleasant, favorable, or [-] bad, distasteful, or unfavorable. We can respond, we can act upon, each sensation and perception, in one of two ways: advance or retreat. We can advance to something to embrace it [+] or to destroy it [-]; we can retreat from something in awe [+] or in danger [-]. In this way, emotion leads directly to physical action.

In life, we seek equilibrium and balance [o], but are plagued by a central nervous system in touch with our surroundings. This is the human dilemma. So great is the desire for equilibrium [o], that the Buddha warned of The Three Poisons — desire, aversion, and ignorance. For the Buddha, ignorance led us to perceive everything as either [+] or [-]. While desire and aversion may be poisons for people on a religious path, they are the life-blood of the creative actor. Sensation and perception may be fundamental obstacles to our human desire for equilibrium, but they are keys to the actor's desire for truthful action. For the actor, unlike the monk, ignorance is a lack of sensitivity to the subtle [+] and [-] messages being sent to our brain.

When a thought, sight, or sound hits us, we sense it, perceive it as [+] or [-], and spontaneously act upon the sensation and perception. Emotion results from strong sensations and perceptions. Hearing a song with past associations can bring tears to our eyes. An old photo in an album can trigger instant laughter. Disequilibrium is necessary for pleasure, as well as pain! Like sensations, people are either a helpful ally [+] or a hindering enemy [-] to the accomplishment of the specific objective of the moment.

Psychologists call spontaneous emotional action like this "acting out", and teach dysfunctional clients strategies and techniques to diffuse emotional impulses through talk. So, in a strange way, learning to act for the stage is unlearning (or at least suspending) psychologically healthy behavior. Unlike well-adjusted citizens, actors on stage act upon their emotions first, and talk about what happened later.

Even imaginary, or old, perceptions can produce genuine emotion, if enough sensory detail is engaged. Daydreaming, fantasizing, and remembering can lead to real emotion. Imagining an audition can lead to actual fear. Anticipating an evening with another person can lead to genuine sexual arousal. Recalling the loss of a loved one can bring a real lump to the throat.

The ability to stimulate emotion in oneself is an important technique for the actor. Prior to each entrance, an actor should "fill up" with the emotion he or she believes the character then holds. Once onstage, however, the actor pursues an objective and allows the emotion to take care of itself, to "happen." Like sweat, emotion flows along, transforming, as the inner stream of emotional consciousness.

Emotion resides in our specific memories. Everything that has happened to us is permanently recorded, through our senses, into our brains. **EMOTIONAL MEMORY RECALL** can be an effective way to fill oneself prior to entering the stage. To re-experience a specific emotion, you need only begin to recall the specific sensory details of the original experience in as great a detail as possible. Gradually, you should feel yourself reacting to the conjured images.

The possibility for emotion can be increased in several ways. First, an actor can "raise the stakes." Actors are more animated by, and audiences prefer to see, life or death intentions. Make choices about your intentions and circumstances which increase the sense of urgency. Want what you want *now*!

Second, effective phrasing of the intention can help increase your emotional involvement in the action. When playing, use the first person singular pronoun "I" when referring to the agent of the action. Also, choose active rather than passive verbs. Passive verbs use the "to be" infinitive. And, when selecting active verbs, avoid dull verbs, or verbs which simply indicate general action, like "to tell," "to inform," "to question," "to ask," or "to show." The formula is :

"I want" + active verb + object.

If you happen to begin with a passive understanding, such as "I want to be happy," think of what would bring about that state of happiness. You might conclude that "I want to cheer up Mary" or "I want to arouse guilt in Tom." You should transform general passive desires into specific active intentions.

Third, seek ways to increase your emotional investment in your action. Eliminate the adverb "just" from the phrasing of your intention. "I just want to convince you to give me a hug" should be rephrased as "I must convince you to give me a hug." Think in terms of superlatives. Your partner is not "okay," but either the "best" or the "worst." It would not "be nice" if you could learn if your partner is telling the truth, but your "life depends upon" determining if the partner is telling the truth. And finally, whomever you encounter is either exactly whom you were looking for, or the last person you wanted to meet. Think superlatively to feel superlatively. The more compelling your attitude, the more compelling your actions.

When beginning actors read scripts and see stage directions like "crying" or "angry" after their characters' names, they often err in their reaction. The note does not mean that the actors should try to wring the noted emotions from themselves at that moment. Rarely do people try to cry or to display genuine anger. Usually the opposite is the case. There are, however, times when people want *to convince* others that they are crying or angry. Words like "crying" and "angry," when describing genuine emotion rather than the appearance of emotion, are more appropriately considered by the other actors on stage; *their* actions should arouse anger or tears in a particular actor. When you see notes describing your character's emotion, first decide if your character wants *to appear* to have that emotion. If so, then the character's objective is known. If the character doesn't want to appear angry or crying, then the note belongs more appropriately to the other characters. Their objectives are then known — to make you cry or to anger you.

As a character, the actor should consider three situations involving emotion:

> 1. The emotion the character holds and brings onto the stage during an entrance.
>
> 2. The emotion the character wishes to convey to whomever is encountered on stage after entering. This emotion can be different from the first.
>
> 3. The emotion the character wishes to generate in the other characters.

These three situations replicate the ways we consider our emotions in everyday life.

☞ 7. Repeat the commonplace activities you have been working on, with properties, observations, and intentions. In this repetition, actors should begin only after filling up offstage with a particular emotion.

MONOLOGUES

All speech springs from an inner stream of mental action. When silent, the inner monologue is called thought. When spoken aloud, the inner stream is called speech. A monologue is a series of uninterrupted short statements. It is what one ends up with after speaking for a while without a verbal response from a listener. People speak for a response. Once they get one, or when they get one they don't want, they adapt.

Actors should begin a monologue **AS IF** they needed to say only one thing to get the response they sought. When "something happens," they go on to the next utterance. The "something" is usually called "feedback," a non-verbal response to what is said. **Nothing** is still feedback; nothing is a non-verbal response indicating that the speaker didn't get through to the listener. Actors wait for feedback before proceeding with verbal actions which end up as a monologue.

☞ 8.   Stand before a partner and say "What a Day!" Unburden your mind and heart, exploring the feelings the day's events produced in you. Discuss how everything has contributed to your present mood. Your partner should participate by engaging you in the Repetition Exercise.

☞ 9.   Repeat Exercise 8 with you and a partner both sharing your days and engaging in the Repetition Exercise. Seek to connect your day with what your partner is saying.

☞ 10. Repeat Exercise 9, after doing emotional preparations.

☞ 11. Repeat Exercise 10 while doing your activities.

☞ 12. Stand before a partner and tell a made-up fairy tale or myth as dramatically as possible. Your partner should participate by engaging you in the Repetition Exercise.

☞ 13. Repeat Exercise 12 with both you and a partner both sharing your fables and engaging in the Repetition Exercise. Seek to connect your fable with what your partner is saying.

☞ 14. Repeat Exercise 13, after doing emotional preparation.

☞ 15. Repeat Exercise 14 while doing your activities.

☞ 16. Repeat Exercise 15, with one actor helping the other

actor with the activity; with one actor trying to stop the other activity.

Monologues, like stories, need feedback. Throughout the history of the theater, actors have been left alone on stage to share the moment with the audience. For a brief time, the audience became the actor's needed confidante.

However, in the nineteenth century, actors changed the conventions, or rules, for performing monologues. The advent of psychology and the introduction of Realistic and Naturalistic drama to the theater repertoire caused the theater's "fourth wall" to move from behind the audience to a position along the proscenium arch, between the actors and the audience. In the Realistic/Naturalistic theater, performance conventions insisted that the actors pretend the audience was not there, and then asked the audience to pretend that the actors did not know that the audience was there. As a result, monologues had to be re-motivated. Monologues could not be moments when the actor spoke with the audience, because there was no audience! Instead, monologues became moments when actors began to speak their innermost thoughts aloud, while alone.

The modern theater has returned the fourth wall to its historical position behind the audience. Consequently, today's actors are free to acknowledge and speak directly with the audience once again. However, some directors may still insist on playing monologues under the old "Peeping Tom" conventions of the nineteenth century.

TEXTS

Beginning actors are often encouraged to "make the words your own." This means that your utterance of memorized words should have the same characteristics as the words you say spontaneously.

☞ 17. Memorize five to ten sentences from a book of interviews. Studs Terkel's (1912–) books provide good material.[7] Memorize the words neutrally or flat, devoid of character, intention, or emotion. Know them backwards and forwards. Sit facing another actor and begin the "What a Day!" Exercise. The other actor should repeat as the Repetition Exercise begins. After a while, slide into the memorized text in whatever mood or attitude your recollection has produced. Your goal should be to blur the distinction between spontaneous speech and memorized text, without altering the memorized text. If, at any point, the repeating actor is not convinced, or does not believe the speaker, the speaker must go back and repeat until the listener believes or is convinced.

☞ 18. Repeat Exercise 17, this time with both actors recalling things from their day, sliding into memorized texts, and repeating. Seek to connect your recollections and memorized text to what you are hearing from your partner.

☞ 19. Repeat Exercise 17, using only the memorized texts, after each actor has "filled up" emotionally.

☞ 20. Repeat Exercise 17 with the actors also engaged in their activities.

☞ 21. Repeat Exercise 17, with both actors engaged in the same activity.

☞ 22. Memorize the lines for a character in Open Scene 1 or 2 (found in Appendix 2) **AS IF** a monologue. Perform the Open Scene with a partner, after filling with a strong emotion, repeating until something happens to make you go on, and while engaged in your activity.

☞ 23. Play the Open Scene again, but this time repeating *silently*. Wait until something happens to make you go on, but realize that **nothing** can be, and often is, "something" to perceive to make you go on. Also, "something" can happen to make you go on in the middle of the other actor's line; you do not need to be polite by waiting until the other actor is finished. Say your line when you must, even if it interrupts or overlaps the other actor. For example, B might feel like saying "I'm serious," after hearing only the words "You can't." If so, B can either say the words, or begin to say the words, but "tread water" with silent repetitions of "I'm serious," until A finishes with the words "mean it."

☞ 24. Repeat Exercise 22, with both actors engaged in one of the activities. If at any point the repeating actor is not convinced or does not believe the speaker, the speaker must go back and repeat until the listener believes or is convinced.

PROJECTION AND PRESENCE

Most acting students have seen more imitation on screens and video monitors than they have on stages. The colored lights which create the illusion of living human beings are manipulated by camera operators and sound engineers. Stage actors need to learn how to fill their spaces with body and voice and to project their presences without the aid of electronic devices.

Most film and video images are of "people" close together in two-shots (two people visible in one frame) or in head shots of one actor. In this way the focus of the audience is directed by the editor. On stage, actors need to direct their audiences' attention by themselves. On stage, actors need to maintain at least an eight foot distance from one another in order to be perceived as individuals. Consequently, actors should work to move away from one another and to only come together briefly for climactic moments.

Actors who maintain their distances appear to be filling their spaces in much the same way tennis players fill theirs. The audience moves its attention to the actor with the "ball"; the actors' "ball" is the more compelling action. A tennis audience watches the ball as it is hit or missed; this is more compelling than watching the player who has just hit the ball. Theatre audiences watch what is most interesting also. So, given two commonplace activities, the audience will gravitate to the one which requires more concentration by the actor. So, given two actors performing equally difficult activities, the audience will attend to the actor speaking. And the audiences' attention will move to actors who need to achieve their objectives the most, for whom the "the stakes are highest."

☞ 25. Repeat Exercise 22 with the actors beginning the scene at least two feet apart. Come together only briefly when necessary and then seek to return to the eight foot distance.

☞ 26. Repeat exercise 23 with the actors beginning the scene at least eight feet apart. Come together only briefly when necessary and then seek to return to the eight foot distance.

☞ 27. Repeat Exercise 24 with the actors beginning the scene at least two feet apart. Come together only briefly when necessary and then seek to return to the eight foot distance.

☞ 28. Repeat Exercise 22 with the actors beginning the scene together. Seek reasons to move eight feet away from one another, coming together only briefly when necessary.

☞ 29. Repeat Exercise 23 with the actors beginning the scene together. Seek reasons to move eight feet away from one another, coming together only briefly when necessary.

☞ 30. Repeat Exercise 24 with the actors beginning the scene together. Seek reasons to move eight feet away from one another, coming together only briefly when necessary.

By maintaining the eight foot distance, actors find they need to automatically increase the volume of their voices in order to be heard by the other actor. This allows them to be more audible to the audience as well.

The performance of the Open Scene illustrates several important points. First, there are no right or wrong ways of performance, only more or less effective, or compelling, choices. Second, texts need actors to give them meaning; only through doing the actions in the here-and-now, listening, and responding, does meaning arise. Third, the Open Scene reveals that a stage character exists only in a particular actor at a particular moment in a particular place. The "identity" of a character exists only when the character has finished his or her actions. "Character" is the summary impression we make after witnessing a series of actions. The German philosopher Arthur Schopenhauer (1788–1860) noted that a person's life tends to make sense only after he or she is dead. Likewise, characters in plays are only understood and known after we have finished the play.

SUBSTITUTION

Like people, characters occasionally reveal their fantasies or memories. Both fantasies and memories have emotional dimensions. To increase the emotional richness of the revelations, actors can substitute their own specific sensory images for the character's words. For example, if the character speaks of "the green fields," before you utter the words, visualize as specifically as possible particular green fields that you yourself saw on a particular occasion. Engage all of your senses by recalling the temperature, the wind, the sounds, and anything else your stream of recall brings to mind. Or, if the character says "I wept," you should visualize in great detail a particular occasion from your past in which you wept. This technique is known as **SUBSTITUTION**.

For example, if you were to choose the poem "Evening" by Hilda Doolittle (1886–1961) (H.D.), you might proceed to ask and answer questions in as personal and as specific a manner as possible.

> The light passes
> from ridge to ridge,
> from flower to flower —
> the hypaticas, wide-spread
> under the light
> grow faint —
> the petals reach inward,
> the bluetips bend
> toward the bluer heart
> and the flowers are lost.

"When have I ever seen mountain ridges in evening? If not mountain ridges, what distant wonder of nature have I seen in the evening? What did it look like? Why was I there? What was I smelling? What was I feeling? What was I hearing? Who was there with me? Where was the source of the light which illuminated the event?"

"When have I ever been near hypaticas [hepaticas]? If not hepaticas, then when have I been near liverwort, mayflowers, or other dainty, cup-shaped, early spring flowers, which sometimes bloom under the snow? What did they look like? Why was I near them? What did I smell? What did they feel like? What was I hearing? Who was there with me? Where was the source of light which illuminated the flowers? If I were to closely examine the flowers, what would I see?"

If the stage were a three-dimensional canvas or projection screen, stand and place the mountain ridges around you, remembering to spread your images at least eight feet apart throughout the space. Place the hypaticas near you in this three-dimensional environment of personal, detailed images. Begin to utter the words of the poem, taking time to fully experience each image before speaking. Feel free to walk, kneel, listen, smell, touch, and feel the images around you.

REFERENTIAL MOVEMENT

From the earliest theatrical performances, actors moved toward the things they described. In the classical Greek and Roman theaters, actors moved toward the left exit when referring to the harbor, port, or foreign lands, and toward the right exit when referring to the city or the palace. They moved toward the altar center stage when speaking to or about the gods. In Elizabethan times, actors gestured toward or looked at the ceiling over them when speaking of the heavens, fate, or God. Actors moved toward the exit last used by the character they were speaking about.

Onstage, time exits in space. When lines refer to the past, the present, or the future, actors can focus on or move toward people, places, or objects associated with their past, present, or future. For example, in *The Cherry Orchard* by Anton Chekhov, the seventeen year old Anya says the following lines when revisiting her old home:

> My room, my windows, it's just as if I'd never gone away. I'm home, home! Tomorrow morning I'll get up and run out to the orchard . . . Oh, if only I could fall

asleep! I didn't get one wink of sleep the whole way coming back, I wore myself out worrying.

An actress can locate the past, present, and future in the lines and physicalize the text by moving toward or focusing on a person, object, or place associated with each time:

> **Present:** "My room, my windows, it's just as if I'd never gone away. I'm home, home!"

> **Future:** "Tomorrow morning I'll get up and run out to the orchard . . . Oh, if only I could fall asleep!"

> **Past:** "I didn't get one wink of sleep the whole way coming back. I wore myself out worrying"

Beginning actors sometimes have a difficult time with the silence necessary to fully recreate an image. The urge to get on with things overtakes them. They fear that the audience will either become bored or begin to suspect that the actor has forgotten the words. Instead, beginning actors need to discover that silence and pause are important tools for drawing the audience into the imaginary world of images on the stage. The great American actress Mrs. Fiske (1865–1932) would advise young actors, "Never give an audience anything until they ask for it." The silence of a pause makes them ask.

☞ 31. Select a brief passage from a descriptive poem. Memorize it and say it aloud. Before saying the words describing each image, pause to visualize in great detail a particular image from your own life analogous to that being described. Take as long as possible. Place each image somewhere around you, **AS IF** you were there, now, amid the actual phenomena. Don't pretend anything. Really listen until you hear. Really touch until you feel. Really look until you see. Wait until you sense it before you say it. Then repeat the utterance, again and again, seeking to make the sensation as vivid as possible.

☞ 32. Texts move through a series of discoveries made by the speaker. Each discovery prompts the speaker to say more. Many Americans have a habit of putting the interjections "Like" or "I mean" in their speech as if to announce each discovery. Go back to your poem and insert "like" or "I mean" before each new discovery. A single sentence may have several discoveries.

> The light, like, passes
> from ridge, like, to ridge,
> like, from flower to, like, flower —
> I mean, the hypaticas, like, wide-spread
> like, under the light
> like, grow faint —
> I mean, the petals, like, reach inward,
> I mean, the bluetips, like, bend
> toward the, like, bluer heart
> and, like, the flowers are, like, lost.

Speak the poem in this new form.

☞ 33. Repeat Exercise 32 without the "Likes" and "I means" Use your voice to communicate the discoveries instead with hesitations.

☞ 34. Repeat the poem after filling up with a particular emotion.

☞ 35. Repeat Exercise 33 while performing your commonplace activity.

Texts cannot ever be fully understood until performed. Intentions are often hidden until the actions are done and the words are said. In fact, Edward Gordon Craig (1872–1966), the British stage theoretician, believed a text to be good in proportion to one's inability to appreciate it through reading alone. Constantin Stanislavski came to believe that characters, too, can only be understood through the performance of individual actions.

Remember the lessons of the Open Scene and Substitution Exercises as you move on to more famous, and more detailed, texts. The temptation to "do it right" increases when a "real" script is in hand. Even if he has never read or seen the play, an actor comes to *Hamlet*, for example, with certain expectations, assumptions, and preconceptions. Likewise, the stage descriptions of Amanda Wingfield in *The Glass Menagerie* can pressure the actress to limit her choices and explorations to the parameters outlined by Tennessee Williams. You need to free yourself from all of these artificial barriers to creative exploration.

Stage directions arrived with the printing press. The French playwright Pierre Corneille (1606–84), one of the first playwrights to print his works, hoped the inclusion of stage directions would limit the actors imaginations. Corneille represents the type of playwright who distrusts actors and directors. The other type of playwright realizes that the plays, if any good, will be produced in circumstances beyond imagination. Sensible playwrights realize that their notes are but suggestions based on the type of auditorium, setting, actors, and costumes living in their minds' eyes as they compose; knowing they could not ever envision all eventualities, playwrights offer possibilities rather than set rules. The American playwright Ronald Ribman (1932–) tells of a note in one of his plays which described how a certain property was pre-set; an over-cautious actor interpreted the note as a direction for his character. The playwright was horrified to see the character pre-set the property as part of the action! Actors need to take stage directions with a grain of sand. Many notes come from stage managers' promptbooks or directors' scripts. Some notes are added by the publisher's editor to assist the general reader's visualization of the action. With such dubious authorship, stage directions are best considered briefly and then put away.

You need to free yourself from artificial barriers to creative exploration. Some actors go so far as to black or white out the stage directions. They prefer to see the words to be said, and trust that the same process which illuminated the Open Scene and Substitution Exercises will illuminate every role, however great, or specifically proscribed.

CHARACTER ANALYSIS

"It wasn't in her character to do such a thing." "He's a real character!" "Character shouldn't be an issue in this campaign." What are these people talking about? What is "character" anyway?

According to the Greek philosopher Aristotle, the word for "character" comes from the word for "habit." A habit is pattern of behavior learned through repetition. A "real character" is a person with an unusual habit of behavior. A political campaign could focus on a candidate's habitual behavior, whether good (bravery) or bad (lying). A person who has not been seen with violent actions as part of her habitual behavior would not be expected to do a violent action.

Actors reveal character on stage as people reveal character in daily life — by doing and saying things so as to create a pattern of behavior. Playwrights assign words and actions to doers of the words and actions. When these words and actions recur, they create a pattern of behavior — a habit — and character is revealed and created. By inventing ways of saying the playwright's words, ways of doing the plot's necessary actions, and by discovering additional actions in rehearsal, actors finish the revelation and creation of character begun by the playwright. As the saying goes,

> Thoughts become words,
> Words become actions,
> Actions become habit,
> Habit becomes character,
> And character becomes destiny.

Great plays reveal the way people are. The English poet Percy Bysshe Shelley (1792–1822) believed that the dramatic art teaches "the human heart the knowledge of itself." That knowledge is not always pleasant.

This guide began by noting differences between human beings and other species. Great plays acknowledge the differences — the ability to reason, analyze, decide, and act altruistically. But great plays also admit the commonality of behavior among all living things. Great plays present both our unique capacities as human beings and our links to the animal world. As a result, actors need to remember that their task is to portray humans as they are, alas, not as they ought to be. We develop as Wild Men and Wild Women to truthfully portray the great range of human experience.

Anthropologists point out two important animal traits underlying the wildness of our human actions — the desire for sexual satisfaction and the instinct for aggression. Today, conservatives seem to have trouble with art which focuses on the former, while liberals have trouble with plays about the latter. Responsible actors follow the truth about human action wherever it may lead them. In fact, the great American drama critic George Jean Nathan (1882–1958) identified the insidious nature of the dramatic art in human history:

> It has always been the mission of the theater to reduce, in so far as it lay within its power, the manners and morals of the community....[F]or the accomplishment, if perhaps not always the intention, of all art is the lowering of human virtue, in the commonly accepted sense of the word, and the conversion of [people] from Methodism to metaphysical and emotional Paganism.[8]

Socially responsible, ethically upright, personally sensitive, and politically correct characters usually inhabit great comedies, as the butt of ridicule and the object of laughter. Great dramas feature well-intentioned people, like ourselves: flawed people in circumstances which provoke, on occasion, socially irresponsible, ethically hypocritical, personally insensitive, and politically incorrect action. In our heart of hearts, we know our weaknesses and limitations; important theater soothes us with the knowledge that we are not alone as Wild Men and Women.

Unlike people in life, characters in plays are teleologically conceived. In other words, characters are made to fulfill a specific function in a particular artificial plot, the end of which is preconceived.

The characters in plays do certain prescribed verbal and physical actions. However, these actions are but the tip of the performance iceberg. Most actions are invented in rehearsal. But whatever their origins, all actions must have motivations and justifications which are 1) inherent in the text itself, 2) suggested by the director in rehearsal, or 3) invented by actors in their creative imaginations.

The source of your character inventions is you. As the American actor Marlon Brando (1924–) wrote:

> People often say that an actor 'plays' a character well, but that's an amateurish notion....In acting everything comes out of what you are or some aspect of *who you* are. Everything is a part of your experience. We all have a spectrum of emotions in us. It is a broad one, and it's the actor's job to reach into this assortment of emotions and experience the ones that are appropriate for his character and his story.[9]

As you read a play, ask the same questions you ask in life. Especially ask "Why?" "Why could the character do or say this at this particular time?" "What could be done to motivate or justify this action or these words?" Don't stop with your first answer. Keep trying new ideas, even ones you think are wrong or stupid. Often bad ideas in the mind become exciting actions in performance. Answers often arise in the spontaneous give and take of a scene, as actors adapt to both their dynamic transforming inner stream of emotional consciousness and the behavior of the other actors. In performance, do not insist on demonstrating your answers; rather, pursue your objectives, while remaining open to the possibility of discovering new strategies to attain them. You may even discover new objectives through playing.

The actor has a unique perspective on a character. The actor is inside looking out. With this special vantage point, come certain obligations. First, you must see only what the character sees. Second, you must see things as the character sees them. Personally, you may see other things, or view things differently than the character. But in the theater, the actor is the character's advocate, not the character's judge. Like a defense attorney, you have the responsibility of presenting the character's case, and letting the audience decide if they like or dislike the character and his or her actions. Like the defense attorney, your goal is to hide your personal opinion of the character's actions. Advocating abnormal behavior is difficult. Psychotherapist Susan Bauer observes that "to adopt anyone's condition as my own is to agree to live among the vulnerabilities that shadow every life. It is to know that there is no way for anyone to sail home in safety."[10]

Your first impression of the character is very important. There will be some aspects of the character which you will like and other aspects you will dislike. Your goal is to understand and reshape the aspects you dislike into one's you can advocate. For example, at first, an actress may consider Amanda Wingfield "domineering" and "manipulative." Later, the actress presents her as "protective" and "helpful." At first, Hamlet could be seen as "indecisive" and "weak." Later, the actor plays him as "cautious" and "sensitive." Medea's goal is not "to do barbaric acts," but rather "to make my husband suffer as much as he as made me suffer." Iago's goal is not "to entertain myself with random acts of hatred," but rather "to punish Othello for selecting an idiot as his lieutenant and for raping my wife." Even if you were to play Hitler, you would need to seek an objective you could advocate. (Remember, Eva Braun found something to love about him. And even Cambodia's tyrant Pol Pot had a wife.) As Aristotle observed, it is most interesting to see characters as people like us: people running into trouble by seeking to do good. Few, if any, of us would do something if we could not justify it. Lady Macbeth loved her husband and wanted only the best for him.

Begin with first things. Why does the character have the name it does? Why is Hamlet named Hamlet? Why is Amanda Wingfield named Amanda Wingfield? What expectations, assumptions, and responsibilities come with the name? Name dictionaries can be helpful.

Next, consider where the character has been prior to the first entrance. What has been happening to Hamlet before he appears at the court and says, "A little more than kin, and less than kind"? What has

Amanda's life consisted of before she is heard calling "Tom?" in Tom's "memory," as he calls the play?

What prompts the character to enter? How does the character feel? What does the character hope to accomplish with his or her first words? Whom does the character expect to find upon entering? What does the character feel toward them? Are they allies or enemies to the character's fulfillment of his or her intention? How does the character want them to feel? After he or she enters, what keeps the character here? What does the character need from the other characters? What is the character getting from them? Finally, why does the character leave? Where is he or she going? What does the character plan to do there?

Repeat this basic analysis for each of the character's appearances onstage. Note the time and place of each of the character's appearances. Time of day, day of the week, and month of the year can all influence action. Also, attend to where the character is. Place can affect behavior: Is the character playing "at home" or "away"? What are the home court advantages?

HEIGHTENED DICTION

Characters in plays will use words and phrases which we do not use in our everyday lives. Throughout history, characters in plays have spoken differently from people in everyday life. Characters may even speak verse or employ what are known as **VERBAL CONCEITS** — linguistic and rhetorical devices or figures of speech. The American playwright and critic Eric Bentley (1916–) maintains that the "primary pleasure of dramatic dialogue [is] the pleasure of perfect articulateness. Nothing pertinent is left unexpressed. Each speaker says all he should say, and says it perfectly — according to the kind of perfection that is appropriate to the context, be it witty and concise or poetic and elaborate....For generally speaking, the drama has room only for proficient talkers."[11]

Nevertheless, actors must choose the language in the same way they choose their own words and phrases in everyday life. If straightforward, common people choose straightforward, common language, then complicated and unusual people must choose complicated and uncommon diction. No less an authority on the power of language than Malcolm X (1925–65) acknowledged the necessity for linguistic study: "I saw that the best thing I could do was get hold of a dictionary — to study, to learn some words."[12]

Playwrights give unusual, unnatural, poetical, complicated, clever, and elevated language deliberately to characters who choose, at a particular moment, to employ unusual, poetical, complicated, clever, or elevated language because that language is the best way the characters know to express what they mean, to achieve their objectives. If a character switches from prose to poetry, ask "Why would that character choose to switch to poetry?" In Shakespeare's *Much Ado About Nothing*, Beatrice speaks in prose until she overhears Benedict declare his love for her; then she speaks only poetry. If a character comes up with a terrible rhyme, ask "Why would that character choose a terrible rhyme?" If a character chooses an old-fashioned or melodramatic phrase, ask "Why would that character choose an old-fashioned, melodramatic phrase?" If a word or sentence is difficult to say, say it as if you chose to say a difficult word or sentence. Stage diction must always be motivated from within the character, and never glided over as a "convention of the time." The audience lives in only one time — now.

Characters choose their words and verbal conceits. Actors need to know the verbal conceits characters may choose:

Alliteration is the repetition of initial or medial consonants in adjacent words. For example, in *The Glass Menagerie* Amanda describes herself as "**p**ossessed of a **p**retty **f**ace and a graceful **f**igure."

Assonance is the repetition of similar vowel sounds in adjacent words. In *The Glass Menagerie*, Amanda reminds her son that "human beings are supposed to chew their food before they swallow it down."

Antithesis is the juxtaposition of contrasting ideas, often in a parallel structure. Tom opens *The Glass Menagerie* with an antithesis: "But I am the opposite of a stage magician. He gives you *illusion* that has the appearance of *truth*. I give you *truth* in the pleasant disguise of *illusion*."

Metaphor is the comparison of two unlike things that, nevertheless, have something in common. In *The Glass Menagerie* Tom uses a metaphor to describe the family's economic situation: "so they were having their fingers pressed down on the fiery Braille alphabet of a dissolving economy."

Onomatopoeia is the use of words whose sound echoes the sense. Tom charges Amanda with addressing "your hawK-liKe aTTention To every biTe I TaKe."

Pun is a play on words. Laura recalls one involving her nickname: "I said *pleurosis* — he thought I said *Blue Roses*." (Notice the antithesis between "I said" and "he thought," as well.)

Repetition is the deliberate echo of a specific word or phrase, though perhaps with a difference. An exchange between Tom and his mother illustrates the verbal conceit:

> AMANDA: Where do you go to, nights?
> TOM: I -**go to** the movies.
> AMANDA: Why do you **go to the movies** so much, Tom?
> TOM: I **go to the movies** because — I like adventure. Adventure is something I don't have **much** of at work, so **I go to the movies**.
> AMANDA: But, Tom, you **go to the movies** entirely too **much.**

Rhyme is the correspondence of the terminal sounds of words.

Simile is a metaphor which uses the word "like." Amanda claims Tom has a "Temperament **like** a Metropolitan star!"

When working on complicated characters, actors should expect complicated verbal pyrotechnics. Consider Hamlet's first scene, his first line:

A little *more* than kin, and *less* than kind.

The line contains an antithesis between "more" and "less," alliterates the "l" and "k" consonants, and puns with the proverb "The nearer in kin the less in kindness"! His mother, Gertrude, continues the linguistic barrage:

Good Hamlet, **c**ast thy *nightly* **c**olour off,"

She alliterates the "C" consonant, assonates the "I" vowel sound, and puns with the word "nightly," as meaning black clothes of mourning, evening attire, and garb worn by a knight! Hamlet's first extensive speech comes after his mother, Gertrude, rhymes "be" with "thee," and provides Hamlet with an opportunity to create an extensive antithesis on her word "seem":

GERTRUDE: If it *be*,
    Why *seems* it so particular with th**ee**?
HAMLET: **S**eems, madam? N**ay**, it is, I **know** not
    seems.
    '*Tis* **n**ot al**o**ne my ink**y** cl**oa**k, good **m**other,
    Nor customary suits of solemn bla**ck**,
    No, **n**or the fruitful river in the eye,
    Nor the d**ej**ected h**a**vior of the visage,
    Together with all f**o**rms, **m**oods, sh**ow**s of gr**ie**f,
    That can d**e**n**o**te **m**e *truly*. Th**e**se ind**ee**d *s**ee**m*,
    For th**ey** are actions that a *man* might pl**ay**;
    But *I* have that *within* which passeth sh**ow** -
    Th**e**se but the *trappings* and the *suits* of w**oe**.

Hamlet sets what "seems" against what "is," what "shows" against what "truly" is, and mere "man" against himself in antithesis. He concludes by rhyming "they" with "play," and associating, "show" with "woe." Antithesis, repetition, alliteration, assonance, and rhyme all work together on Hamlet's behalf. The character chooses to launch a linguistic attack!

When working on a text with heightened diction, actors should take certain steps. First, identify the uncommon words and verbal conceits. Second, say the text aloud, overplaying the words and phrases identified. Third, notice the emotional attitude expressed by the utterance. As with the Koran, the very act of saying heighten diction aloud produces a particular feeling in the speaker. Finally, ask why could the character choose these particular words and devices? Words are chosen to convey attitudes as well as information. For example, the person who chooses to say "abode" has a different attitude toward his house than the person who chooses to call it a "pad," even though the place is the same. The language chosen is the best way for a particular character to express a particular attitude toward a particular thing in the pursuit of a particular objective.

Specifically chosen words (non-colloquial words, including technical terms, foreign terms, and obsolete or archaic terms) and conceits do particular work for you and need to be "coined" or, as they say at the Royal Shakespeare Company, "fresh-minted" at the moment you utter them. Put quotation marks around the words and say them as quotations. Stage diction must seem to be uttered for the first time no matter how archaic the word or how convoluted the verbal conceit. And relish the heightened diction your character has chosen; if the character didn't love it, other language would have been chosen.

THE SCORE

Whenever a character's intention changes, the character begins a new **UNIT OF ACTION**. If a musician's score is divided into measures, the actor's score is divided into units of action. Each new intention brings new strategies, alliances, obstacles, verbal conceits, and emotional investment. Each new intention marks the beginning of a new unit of action.

Sometimes "playing the opposite" objective or intention can reveal interesting aspects of a character. Opposite emotions usually live side by side in our important human relationships. So, instead of playing "to convince him that I love him," play "to convince him that I hate him." Characters, like human beings, often try counterproductive routes toward their goals. Consistency is as unnatural and unbelievable onstage as it is in life. Logical and clear transitions are equally rare. Embrace the character's contradictions as evidence of lifelikeness. Watch people, and see!

To generate emotion, to "raise the stakes," an actor can discover or invent an obstacle for each intention. As we have noted, struggle focuses concentration. Sometimes the pursuit of an objective by one character is another character's obstacle. For example, Hamlet's desire to learn if the ghost is telling the truth meets an obstacle in Claudius' desire to hide his involvement in Hamlet's father's death. Amanda's desire to find a husband for her daughter meets an obstacle in her son's desire to escape the home. Often a physical obstacle or property can provide a key emotional stimulus to an actor. The skull of Yorik and the glass unicorn can be powerful emotional releases for actors in *Hamlet* and *The Glass Menagerie*. The discovery or invention of obstacles and properties for each unit of action can enrich the acting score.

The analogy between sport and the dramatic theater is important. Playing your objective, shooting at your target, puts you in competition with other actors playing their objectives, shooting at their targets. Play to win! Too many actors are guilty of loitering on stage. Be the first player to hit your target. Do whatever is necessary! "Trying is not enough," as Yoda the Jedi master says; "Try is not. Either do or do not." Some actors get sidetracked into playing other things: actors "play the character" by focusing on convincing us that their limp, fever, or accent is real; actors "play the emotion" by trying to generate and wallow in a particular feeling; actors "play age" by squeaking their voice, shaking their hands, or bouncing around; actors "play the genre" either by trying to make us laugh at everything or by carrying the weight of the world on their shoulders; actors "play the region" by focusing on dialectical accuracy. To mirror life, you must play your objective.

As a musical score has a treble clef and a bass clef, an actor's score has a text and a SUBTEXT. The text is the words themselves on the literal level. The text can be read and studied at home. The subtext is action on the psychological, ulterior level of a relationship. The subtext is what brings an audience to see productions of plays they have seen before. A single printed text can have an infinite variety of possible subtexts. For example, think of how many different ways the three words "I love you" can be said. They can even be uttered to convince us of the opposite! The subtext is what gives life to the Open Scene. The subtext is the focus of the actor's spontaneous exploration in rehearsal.

A musical score often has an overriding theme which gives unity to the piece. Similarly, an actor's score has a SUPEROBJECTIVE, a consuming desire which both unites and subsumes all of the character's individual intentions. Hamlet's superobjective might be to avenge his father's death. Amanda Wingfield's superobjective might be to help her children find happiness in life. Some characters, like Hamlet, attain their objectives; others, like Amanda, fail.

Change is basic to life and to dramatic characters. To better understand how a character changes in the course of a play, actors often measure the character at the beginning of the play against the character at the end of the play. How the character changes is the character's **DEVELOPMENTAL ARC**. The superobjective shapes the character's arc.

The developmental arc, composed of a series of objectives, comprises the actor's performance safety net. In the theatre, as opposed to film or video, each performance is unique, custom-made, susceptible to being either better or worse than ever before. Impulses take the actor into choices never made previously as the character mysteriously begins to play the actor. Actors need to trust the developmental arc and the score they have devised enough to allow themselves to go with the moment. The actress Glenn Close (1947–) describes the phenomenon:

> It's really weird.... The other day, it was just a run-through dress rehearsal, and I think I gave one of the best performances I've ever given in my life. With no audience. And it takes me a couple of days to get over that, because you don't know where it came from. You know that it was something unusual, and you know that you can't do it again if you try intellectually to conjure it up. You can't. So you have to let it all go. It's almost like channeling — what I would presume channeling would be."[13]

Often consideration of a character's **POLAR ATTITUDES** can clarify the arc. In the 1960s, psychologist Eric Berne (1910–70) developed a verbal shorthand — "I'm Okay/You're Okay" — which can help. According to Berne, four possible attitudes toward oneself and others are possible: "I'm [+]/You're [+]," "I'm [+]/You're [-]." "I'm [-]/You're [+]," and "I'm [-]/You're [-]." Your character's disposition at the beginning of the play, and your character's disposition at the end of the play, should be one of these four possibilities. For example, Hamlet's disposition might change from "I'm [-]/You're [-] to I'm [+]/You're [+]." Or Laura Wingfield's might change from "I'm [-]/You're [+]" to "You're [+]/I'm even more [-] than I was."

On stage, the scores of the actor-characters meet and adapt. In performance, actors can **ASSIST** one another. In sports — basketball, hockey, and soccer — when a player does something which leads directly to another player's score, an assist is credited to that player. On stage, an assist is the doing of something which could motivate the other actor's line. For example, if your partner's next line is "I love it when you do that," you could assist in a variety of ways: a kiss, a slap, a caress, a finger. Great actors are known for making others' performances better through the quality and imaginativeness of their assists. As an actor, keep on the look out for the unexpected assist. And when nothing is offered, be prepared to justify your line as a response to "getting nothing." It should still work. In sport, a team with a lot of assists is considered to display team work; in the theatre, a cast with a lot of assists is considered an **ensemble.**

☞ 36. Analyze a character from a realistic play. A realistic play features characters whose actions resemble those of people living in everyday life. Attend to the following considerations:

   1. Significance of name.

   2. Biography prior to first entrance.

   3. Motivation for entrance.

   4. Initial intention.

   5. Strategy to attain intention.

   6. Identification and analysis of verbal conceits.

   7. Obstacle to intention.

   8. Subsequent intentions, strategies, and obstacles.

   9. Reason for exit.

   10. Repeat 3-8 for each entrance.

   11. Identification of superobjective.

   12. Determination of polar attitudes in developmental arc.

☞ 37. Read the lines of your character for each scene as a monologue. Note when intentions seem to change. Play the first unit of action with the other actors in the scene in your own words, repeating each expression until something happens to make you go on.

☞ 38. With the other actors, play the first four lines of your first unit of action as a Repetition Exercise. Wait for something to happen before going on. At the end of the four lines, return to the first line, AS IF in an endless loop. Continue with the scene, adding one line at a time to the Repetition Exercise. Say "I don't believe you" when you don't believe your partner, AS IF it were part of the scene, and continue.

As you improvise and repeat, you will make discoveries which alter your score. An actor's score is a work in progress, a record of what is happening, not a blueprint for what will happen the next time the scene is played.

A REHEARSAL STRATEGY

The technique you are learning can help you prepare a scene without the help of a director. Avoid the temptation to function as a director to your partner; offer no suggestions or advice or insight. Spontaneously adapt to whatever your partner does, assuming that it is deliberate.

1. Memorize the first three or four lines of your character in the scene. With your partner, begin the first line as a repetition exercise. Repeat the line back and forth until something happens to make the next line emerge. Repeat that line until something happens to make the first line reappear. Continue this way through the second line until something happens to bring forth the third line. Repeat the third line from your point of view until something happens to cause the first line to return. Here is how a scene from Dorothy Parker's (1893–1967) *Here We Are* might progress:

The lines read:

> **He:** Oh Yeah? Where did you hear that?
> **She:** He told me so himself?
> **He:** Oh, he told you so himself. I see. He told you so himself.
> **She:** You've got a lot of right to talk about Joe Brooks.

You and your friend Louise. All you ever talk about is Louise.

He: Oh for heaven's sake! What do I care about Louise? I just thought she was a friend of yours, that's all. That's why I even noticed her.

In rehearsal:

He: Oh yeah?

She: Yeah.

He: Oh yeah?

She: Yeah.

He: Where did you hear that?

She: Where did I hear that?

He: Where did you hear that?

She: Where did I hear that?

He: Where did you hear that?

She: He told me so himself.

He: He told you so himself.

She: He told me so himself.

He: He told you so himself.

She: He told me so himself.

He: Oh yeah.

She: Yeah.

He: Oh yeah?

She: Yeah.

He: Where did you hear that?

She: Where did I hear that?

He: Where did you hear that?

She: Where did I hear that?

He: Where did you hear that?

She: He told me so himself.

He: He told you so himself.

She: He told me so himself.

He: He told you so himself.

She: He told me so himself.

He: Oh, he told you so himself.

She: Oh, he told me so himself.

He: Oh, he told you so himself.

She: Yeah.

He: Oh yeah?

She: Yeah.

He: Where did you hear that?

She: Where did I hear that?

He: Where did you hear that?

She: Where did I hear that?

He: Where did you hear that?

She: He told me so himself.

He: He told you so himself.

She: He told me so himself.

He: He told you so himself.

She: He told me so himself.

He: Oh, he told you so himself.

She: Oh, he told me so himself.

He: I see.

She: You see.

He: I see.

She: You see.

He: I see.

She: You see.

He: Oh yeah.

She: Yeah.

He: Oh yeah?

She: Yeah.

He: Where did you hear that?

She: Where did I hear that?

He: Where did you hear that?

She: Where did I hear that?

He: Where did you hear that?

She: He told me so himself.

He: He told you so himself.

She: He told me so himself.

He: He told you so himself.

She: He told me so himself.

He: Oh, he told you so himself.

She: Oh, he told me so himself.

He: I see.

She: You see.

He: I see.

She: You see.

He: I see.

She: You see.

He: He told you so himself.

She: He told me so himself.

He: He told you so himself.

She: He told me so himself.

He: He told you so himself.

She: He told me so himself.

He: He told you so himself.

She: You've got a lot of right to talk about Joe Brooks.

He: I've got a lot of right to talk about Joe Brooks.

She: You don't have a lot of right to talk about Joe Brooks.

He: I've got a lot of right to talk about Joe Brooks.

She: You don't have a lot of right to talk about Joe Brooks.

He: I've got a lot of right to talk about Joe Brooks.

She: You've got a lot of right to talk about Joe Brooks.

He: Oh yeah.

She: Yeah.

He: Oh yeah?

She: Yeah.

He: Where did you hear that?

She: Where did I hear that?

He: Where did you hear that?

She: Where did I hear that?

He: Where did you hear that?

She: He told me so himself.

He: He told you so himself.

She: He told me so himself.

He: He told you so himself.

She: He told me so himself.

He: Oh, he told you so himself.

She: Oh, he told me so himself.

He: I see.

She: You see.

He: I see.

She: You see.

He: I see.

She: You see.

He: He told you so himself.

She: He told me so himself.

He: He told you so himself.

She: He told me so himself.

He: He told you so himself.

She: He told me so himself.

He: He told you so himself.

She: You've got a lot of right to talk about Joe Brooks.

He: I've got a lot of right to talk about Joe Brooks.

She: You don't have a lot of right to talk about Joe Brooks.

He: I've got a lot of right to talk about Joe Brooks.

She: You don't have a lot of right to talk about Joe Brooks.

He: I've got a lot of right to talk about Joe Brooks.

She: You've got a lot of right to talk about Joe Brooks.

He: Me and my friend Louise.

She: You and your friend Louise.

He: My friend Louise.

She: You and your friend Louise.

He: Oh yeah.

She: Yeah.

He: Oh yeah?

She: Yeah.

He: Where did you hear that?

She: Where did I hear that?

He: Where did you hear that?

She: Where did I hear that?

He: Where did you hear that?

She: He told me so himself.

He: He told you so himself.

She: He told me so himself.

He: He told you so himself.

She: He told me so himself.

He: Oh, he told you so himself.

She: Oh, he told me so himself.

He: I see.

She: You see.

He: I see.

She: You see.

He: I see.

She: You see.

He: He told you so himself.

She: He told me so himself.

He: He told you so himself.

She: He told me so himself.

He: He told you so himself.

She: He told me so himself.

He: He told you so himself.

She: You've got a lot of right to talk about Joe Brooks.

He: I've got a lot of right to talk about Joe Brooks.

She: You don't have a lot of right to talk about Joe Brooks.

He: I've got a lot of right to talk about Joe Brooks.

She: You don't have a lot of right to talk about Joe Brooks.

He: I've got a lot of right to talk about Joe Brooks.

She: You've got a lot of right to talk about Joe Brooks.

She: You and your friend Louise.

He: Me and my friend Louise.

She: You and your friend Louise.

He: My friend Louise.

She: You and your friend Louise.

She: All you ever talk about is Louise.

He: All I ever talk about is Louise.

She: All you ever talk about is Louise.

He: All I ever talk about is Louise.

She: All you ever talk about is Louise.

He: All I ever talk about is Louise.

She: All you ever talk about is Louise.

and on and on through the scene or through the play

2. This exercise should suggest an objective the character may be pursuing. Think of ways to translate that objective into a physical objective.

3. Think of activities the character could be doing in this place or at this time. Think of activities which could further the objective and think of activities which would frustrate the objective. Repeat the exercise with a clear physical objective and with a definite activity. Repeat the exercise with different objectives and different activities. Try to make your partner's activity work to further your objective. Remember to keep your distance and to come together only occasionally.

4. Repeat the exercise after filling up with an emotion. Try the scene several times each time with a different emotion. Throughout your experimentation with objectives, activities, and emotional preparations do not discard some ideas, however foolish they may seem, without first trying them out in the exercise. Often a foolish idea becomes a compelling performance when put into play.

5. Review the text, looking for repetitions you could "quote' back to your partner. Highlight them.

> **He:** Oh Yeah? Where did you hear that?
>
> **She:** He told me so himself?
>
> **He:** Oh, *he told you so himself.* I see. *He told you so himself.*
>
> **She:** You've got a lot of right to talk about Joe Brooks. *You* and your friend Louise. All *you* ever *talk about* is *Louise.*
>
> **He:** Oh for heaven's sake! What do I care *about Louise?* I just thought she was a friend of *yours,* that's all. That's why *I* even noticed her.

6. Review your partners lines, looking for internal cues, the first "thing that could happen" which could prompt your reply.

This technique presents an integrated method of preparation. Line memorization, blocking, analysis all occur at the same time.

Beginning actors have similar problems:

- ☹ They don't let their impulse to move have full reign. Contrariwise, they move without purpose, wandering around aimlessly.

- ☹ They are insensitive to things happening which could cause them to go on to their next line. They miss internal cues, always waiting for their partner's line to end before they begin to react.

- ☹ They do things without waiting for something to happen to make them. Take as long as necessary, wait, to observe something or for something to rise up in you to cause you to speak or act.

☹ Too much seems planned. They seem to be playing their analysis and indicating their interpretation.

☹ Their objectives don't have a physical component.

☹ Their emotional preparation before the scene is insufficient. They start the scene without a full tank.

☹ Their objectives are not important enough to them. Raise the stakes.

☹ They try to make odd or archaic words and phrases seem natural rather than deliberating choosing that word or coining that phrase in the moment.

☹ They miss figures of speech, especially repetitions and alliterations. They do not play them as character choices in the moment. Repetitions should be tossed back as in tennis.

☹ They play character's traits (i.e., age or attitude or emotion) rather than their objective.

The checklist of questions in Appendix 3 can both guide your analysis of a character and help you begin your score. After completing the thirty-eight exercises in this section, a young actor[14] wrote the following:

LEARN NOT; DO
Do actions as if they were your own.
Act on instinct, not thought.
Always have a purpose
Let that purpose be the most vital and urgent need you
    could possibly have.
Strive for, and attain everything in the Now.
Listen, and react.
Only speak when the need is there, otherwise,
Let your actions do the speaking.

Communicate to both the actors and the audience.

Believe in yourself.

Believe in your character.

Understand as she would, think only as he would.

Don't be afraid of spontaneity

Always be Real.

Believable will follow.

Fear no obstacles, overcome them.

Don't remember your lines:

Speak them.

Don't pretend to be, that which you are not.

Be only what you know.

Perform only when you know all the answers and are
full of unanswered questions.

VARIATION ONE:

PLAYING VERSE

Humpty Dumpty sat on a wall.
Humpty Dumpty had a great fall.
All the king's horses and all the king's men
Couldn't put Humpty together again.

If you can understand and speak *Humpty Dumpty*, you can understand and speak Shakespearean diction. One of a beginning actor's greatest fears is of confronting poetry. However, you may rest assured that the same principles of verse which characterize the childhood nursery rhyme are used by Shakespeare to create some of the most dynamic stage speech ever uttered.

Action, as they say, precedes utterance. We speak because we cannot attain our goals through physical action alone. But if all speech, as we observed in Part I, is purposeful, then what is the purpose of putting the story of Humpty Dumpty in verse? Why not put the story of Mr. Dumpty in prose, like the stories of Red Riding Hood and Aladdin? Why can't all plays be in prose? What is the purpose of poetic speech, anyhow?

When did you first learn the "Humpty Dumpty" verse? Probably you cannot recall; it may seem you've always known it. On the other hand, can you recall, word for word, something you learned just yesterday? Probably not. And in the reason lies one of the values of verse in the theater: actors can remember it.

Unfortunately, beginning actors are often intimidated by verse. They see complex sentence structures, intricate metaphors, and unusual words; the language is unlike any they have ever heard in everyday life. Their initial reactions can cause beginning actors to err in two basic ways.

First, they can believe that earlier audiences were more familiar with verse, or more educated in verse, or more willing to accept verse on the stage; they may believe that verse was the normal convention for stage diction. With these beliefs, the actors work to make the verse sound beautiful.

Even if these beliefs were correct (any most of them are not), they do not solve the problem of speaking verse for today's audience; the historical audience is not the one for whom today's actor will play. The people who attend rock concerts and chamber concerts, watch "Masterpiece Theater" and "Beavis and Butthead," and listen to Prince (1959–) and Philip Glass (1937–) must find the actors' handling of verse diction not only beautiful, but believable and compelling.

Second, beginning actors can conclude that today's audience would never accept verse as believable. Consequently, they work to make the verse sound like everyday prose dialogue. As a result, the play and the character are lost in the actors' attempt to limit their imaginations.

The British actor Sir John Gielgud (1904–) notes the two paths to verse hell available to the actor:

> Actors are so often unmusical, and often, too the rhythm of the verse turns to a singsong and the meaning is obscured. Or they break up every speech with realistic pauses and breaks to give the illusion of spontaneous thought. This is equally fatal. The phrasing and rhythm and pace should support one, as water does a swimmer, and should be handled with the same skill and pace.[15]

However, for actors who understand verse's function both as an extension of character and as an acting tool, the queer language suddenly becomes the most exciting they have ever studied or performed.

Language is written in verse because it is the best for the playwright and best for the character. It is best for the playwright because through verse the playwright can, though absent, communicate tempo, rhythm, stress, and phrasing to the actors, while physically engaging the audience in the pulse of the drama. The rhythm and meter of stage language, like the rhythm and meter of song lyrics, can generate emotion in both the actor and the audience. As the American composer Virgil Thompson (1896–1989) wrote,

> Actually, I see no reason to deny that the constraints of music, which begin with rhythm and meter and go on to cover all the possible combinations within any harmonic series, are not only structural elements for aiding memory but expressive vocabularies as well. Not dictionaries of emotion, not at all, but repositories of devices for provoking without defining them.[16]

The modern British playwright Ronald Duncan (1914–) chose verse because "I wanted the language to carry the maximum charge ... was watering the vegetable garden. I observed that the intensity of the jet of water was governed by restricting the outlet."[17] Verse is the actor's "restricting outlet" which allows for rapid enunciation without loss of intelligibility. Verse helps the actors because 1) it is easier than prose to memorize and remember; 2) it reveals both distinct traits and powerful objectives of the character; 3) it contains notes from the playwright.

Verse also aids the audience entrance into the rhythm of the play, the situation, and the character. As George T. Wright observes in *Shakespeare's Metrical Art*, "if the actors will keep the meter, our nervous systems can register the continuing metrical pattern even while our more conscious attention is being directed to the action, the character, and the substance of their words and sentences."[18] When actors read the lines as a particular character's chosen means to attain a specific goal involving specific people at a particular moment, they usually find that the resultant stress and accent matches the stress and accent of the verse! *Playwrights write in verse to aid the actors' efforts in understanding their characters, their characters' intentions, and their characters' strategies for attaining their goals.*

POETRY
AND VERSE

One of my students called any speech which deviated from his own way of speaking "screwed up." Poetry is probably the most "screwed up" language of all. Clearly, poetry is a special way of using language. Poetry is, in fact, the art of language. The English playwright Ben Jonson (1572–1637) noted that poetry "speaketh somewhat above a mortal mouth." Poetic diction is **heightened diction** (as discussed in Part I) emanating from a character whose sensibility reaches beyond our everyday existence. George T. Wright continues: "Knowing the direction and tone a speech or scene is to take, the playwright evidently chose to cast it in verse or prose, and in verse or prose of a particular description, because that kind of language was needed to bring out the special intentions he had for this point in the play."[19]

Poetic diction can be either prose or verse. Prose and verse are the two basic modes, or manners, of employing language. Prose is unmetered language; verse is metered language. *Humpty Dumpty* is written in metered language. **Meter** is the inner rhythmical structure of the line. The rhythmical structure of a line is made of a recurring, countable pattern of accented syllables. Consequently, characters may speak prose poetry or verse poetry. For example, in Shakespeare's plays, characters speak prose 28 percent of the time, and verse 72 percent of the time; they choose to rhyme 7 percent of the time they speak verse.

There is some prose poetry which resembles everyday language. In fact, the line between poetry and prose can resemble the line separating the hill from the valley — easier to observe in theory than in reality. Prose poetry seems to result from a more deliberate, a more conscious, selection of precise words, phrases, and sound combinations than the one we choose to use in our everyday living. British poet Samuel Taylor Coleridge (1772–1834) consolidated this perspective when he said that everyday diction sought "words in the best order," while poetry tried to put "the best words in the best order."

When the sounds of language begin to fall into a regular order, as they do in *Humpty Dumpty*, prose becomes **verse**. When sound syllables, energies, durations, or pitches are arranged into a countable pattern, the result is called **verse**. Verse is language in continuous rhythm. *Humpty Dumpty* is verse. The basic unit of verse is the **line**. *Humpty Dumpty* has four lines.

☞ 1. Choose a nursery rhyme or *Jabberwocky* in Appendix 4. Count the number of lines of verse.

☞ 2. Choose a verse monologue by William Shakespeare. Count the number of lines of verse.

SCANSION

In verse, syllables are counted. **Meter** is the inner rhythmical structure of the line of syllables. The English language is based on the accented and unaccented syllables in a line. To **scan** means to count the number of syllables in a line of verse. How many syllables does *Humpty Dumpty* have? Caution: The answer is not immediately available.

☞ 3. Count the number of syllables in your chosen nursery rhyme or *Jabberwocky*.

☞ 4. Count the number of syllables in each line of your chosen monologue by William Shakespeare.

All words have syllables. All languages construct syllables out of vowels and consonants. Consequently, pronunciation is the key to the identification of rhythmic syllables. For example, the words "all," "words," and "have" are made of but one syllable. Other words are multi-syllabic. The word "syllable," for example, is made of three syllables, the first of which [syl] is stressed, or emphasized, in pronunciation.

Playwrights can increase or decrease the number of syllables in words. **Elision** is the blending of two or more sounds into one sound. "I am" become "I'm"; "to us" becomes "tus"; "the effect" becomes "theffect." "Fiddler" or "fiddeler," "augry" or "augury,"; "fire," "flower," "tires," "prayer," and "riot" have all been pronounced as monosyllabic and disyllabic words. Scanning lines of verse lets actors hear playwrights tell them which pronunciations they prefer.

In Shakespeare's *Richard II*, John of Gaunt elides several words:

> Methinks I am a prophet new **inspired** [becomes **inspir'd**]
> And thus, **expiring** [becomes **expi'ring**], do fortell of him.
> His rash, fierce blaze of riot cannot last,
> For **violent** [becomes **vi'lent**] fires soon burn out themselves.
> Small **showers** [becomes **show'rs**] last long, but sudden storms are short.
> He **tires** [becomes **ti'rs**] betimes that spurs too fast betimes.

☞ 5. Identify the words in your chosen nursery rhyme or *Jabberwocky* which have alternate pronunciations with more or less syllables.

☞ 6. Identify the words in your chosen verse monologue which have alternate pronunciations with more or less syllables.

ACCENT
AND RHYTHM

A line of verse is but an organized row of stressed and unstressed syllables. The previous sentence is a line of nineteen syllables. Although the line has stressed and unstressed syllables, it is not verse. To create verse, the sentence would need to be re-ordered to create a **rhythm**, defined as a recurrent accent or beat:

A line of verse is but a row of sounds

☞ 7. Speak the above line without any stress whatsoever. Then speak the sentence three times, each time with a different meaning. Notice how different meanings change where the stresses fall.

Verse allows the playwright to limit the possible meanings by transforming the natural stresses of pronunciation into artificial units called **feet**. A **foot**, the smallest bit of rhythmic language, is an accented syllable plus one or more unaccented syllables.

$$x \quad ' \quad x \quad ' \quad x \quad ' \quad x \quad ' \quad x \quad '$$
[A line] [of verse] [is but] [a row] [of sounds]

Accent differs from **stress**. Stress is natural speech emphasis; accent is the emphasis assigned a syllable due to its placement in a foot. **There is only one accent in each foot.**

Each foot has a definite arrangement of stressed and unstressed syllables. Conventionally, "x" marks an unaccented syllable and " ' " denotes an accented syllable. Though there are dozens of foot types, the American poet Edgar Allan Poe (1809–49) believed any verse could be scanned as one of the following five basic types:

x	'		
de	lay		
a	lone	[x ']	iamb
sub	mit		

'	x		
sea	son		
win	dow	[' x]	trochee
ta	ble		

```
    x    x      '
    se  ven  teen              [ x x ' ]   anapest


    x    '    x
    re  mem  ber               [ x ' x ]   amphibrach


    '    x    x
    fla  ter  y                [ ' x x ]   dactyl
```

When you scan a line of verse, you give each syllable either an accent mark ['] or an non-accent mark [x].

Iambic verse is the most common in English. Iambic verse is made of iambs. "A line of verse is but a row of sounds" is a line of iambic verse:

```
    x    '    x    '    x    '    x    '    x    '
    [A line] [of verse] [is but] [a row] [of sounds]
```

Trochaic verse is the next most frequent form. "How can I begin to read this drivel" is a line of trochaic verse:

```
    '    x    x x    '    x    x    x    '    x
    [How can] [I be] [gin to] [read this] [dri vel]
```

When looking at a line of verse, first note where the stresses fall naturally. **Humpty Dumpty sat on a wall.** "Hump," "Dump," "sat," and "wall" are stressed in the first line or sentence. Add another sentence: **Humpty Dumpty had a great fall.** In this sentence, the same pattern of stressed and unstressed syllables is repeated, with stresses on 'Hump', "Dump," "had," and "fall." Each line or sentence has four stressed syllables.

☞ 8.   Scan your chosen nursery rhyme or *Jabberwocky*, noting where stresses fall naturally. Identify the simple subject, verb, and object of each sentence.

☞ 9.   Scan your chosen nursery rhyme or *Jabberwocky* to

give each syllable either an accent or a non-accent mark.

☞ 10. Scan your chosen verse monologue, noting where stresses fall naturally. Identify the simple subject, verb, and object of each sentence.

☞ 11. Scan your chosen verse monologue to give each syllable either an accent or a non-accent mark.

Each syllable in *Humpty Dumpty* is part of a foot, the basic unit of speech, containing one accented syllable and at least one unaccented syllable. Each line of *Humpty Dumpty* has the same foot pattern:

(' x x) (' x x) (' x x) (' x x).

The ten voiced syllables in each of the first two lines is followed by an unvoiced two beat rest, or **caesura**. The final foot of the first two lines requires the speaker to silently "think" two additional syllables before moving one to the next line.

$$
\begin{array}{cccc}
{}^{\prime}\ \ \text{x}\ \ \text{x} & {}^{\prime}\ \ \text{x}\ \text{x} & {}^{\prime}\ \ \text{x}\ \ \text{x} & {}^{\prime}\ \ \text{x}\ \text{x} \\
\end{array}
$$
[Hum pe ty] [Dum pe ty] [sat on a] [wall __ __]

$$
\begin{array}{cccc}
{}^{\prime}\ \ \text{x}\ \ \text{x} & {}^{\prime}\ \ \ \text{x}\ \text{x} & {}^{\prime}\ \ \text{x}\ \ \text{x} & {}^{\prime}\ \ \text{x}\ \text{x} \\
\end{array}
$$
[Hum pe ty] [Dum pe ty] [had a great] [fall __ __]

Humpty Dumpty is made of feet of three syllables. Each foot accents the first syllable; this kind of foot is called a **dactyl**. And because a line with four feet is considered written in **tetrameter**, the verse form of *Humpty Dumpty* is known as **dactylic tetrameter**.

☞ 12. Divide each line of your chosen nursery rhyme or *Jabberwocky* into feet. Note any caesuras. Identify the verse form.

☞ 13. Divide each line of your chosen verse monologue into feet. Note any caesuras. Identify the verse form.

ANALYZING THE VERSE

All English verse is, like *Humpty Dumpty*, characterized by a pattern of regular lines of recurring numbers of accented syllables. Most actors will have their first encounter with verse in the plays of William Shakespeare. When reading Shakespeare's verse, first note where the stresses fall naturally and the pattern which the stresses create. Pronounce the words as we normally do. Occasionally, you will discover that consistency of pattern might require an old-fashioned pronunciation. You must then choose between having a fluid verse line and a recognizable word. Most actors find that a recognizable word is what their characters would use, although some characters in some situations might elect an alternative pronunciation.

People in Shakespeare's day interacted through speech more than through writing. Consequently, their listening and speaking skills were more developed and sensitive than ours are. We rely more on printed words and visual images for our information than did people of the past. Most people (and certainly most actors) were illiterate, but compensated with an extraordinary ability to remember detailed messages after just one hearing. Verse facilitated their need to hear and remember accurately.

Shakespearean verse exploits English-speakers' natural tendency to pronounce words by alternating stressed and unstressed, accented and unaccented, syllables. Since the most important part of a sentence is the verb, it receives emphasis through a simple iamb, for example: "Will wrote." The iamb's accent tells us **what** happened; to reverse the natural accent tendency and pronounce a trochee, would tell us **who** did it. The natural English accent tendency also automatically subordinates adjective to noun. "Long speech." The natural stress pattern reinforces the general rule that adjectives are less important than the words they modify and that they should be stressed only to contrast one noun with another. In all cases, English places the more important word after the less important word: "walk fast," "is hard," "on stage." Accent echoes the natural tendency of English to be climactic.

Shakespeare wrote most of his lines in **iambic pentameter**, commonly called **blank verse**. But not always. Some lines have more, and some lines have less, than five measures. Some measures are not iambs. But when Shakespeare varies his form, it is always deliberate, always for a particular reason, and always based on a particular character's particular choice at a particular moment in the action.

The analysis of Shakespearean verse follows the same method as the analysis of *Humpty Dumpty*. For example, in William Shakespeare's *The Tempest*, the goddess Ceres sings a song with natural stresses:

> Vines with clustring branches growing,
>
> Plants with goodly burden bowing.

After finding the natural stresses, locate the feet:

> [Vines with] [clustring] [branches] [growing]
>
> [Plants with] [goodly] [burden] [bowing]

Each foot is a **trochee**. And since each line has four feet, the verse form is **trochaic tetrameter**.

Natural stress does not always coincide with metrical accent, however. In playwright John Ford's (1586–1640) *The Broken Heart*, Orgilus introduces the following song. (The natural stresses are noted.)

> Oh no more, no more, too late
>
> Sighes are spent; the burning Tapers
>
> Of a life as chaste as Fate,
>
> Pure as are unwritten papers,
>
> Are burnt out: no heat, no light
>
> Now remaines; 'tis ever night.

Scansion of the song reveals that meter and accent ignore word importance and pause.

[Oh no] [more, no] [more, too] [late   ]

[Sighes are] [spent; the] [burning] [Tapers]

[Of a] [life as] [chaste as] [Fate,   ]

[Pure as] [are un] [written] [papers,]

[Are burnt] [out: no] [heat, no] [light   ]

[Now re] [maines; 'tis] [ever] [night.   ]

The verse form is again trochaic tetrameter, but with many interesting features. Several lines lack the final unaccented syllable. Ford thereby signals to the actor that a pause in these places may be effective.

Scansion reveals the dynamic tension between natural stress and metrical pattern which energizes verse on stage in a way unavailable to prose. Once the speech's metrical pattern is recognized through scansion, it remains in the actors' subconscious as a rhythmic pattern of expectation, ready to "resolve ambiguous syllables in its favor, and able at times to overcome the slight reluctance of an occasional phrase to take the required shape."[20]

To summarize the technique for analyzing the verse:

1. Note the words everyday pronunciation would stress.

2. Note the simple subject, verb, and object in each sentence, observing if the natural stress falls on them; focusing on subject, object, and verb paradoxically increases intelligibility while at the same time enlivening the verse.

3. Divide the line into feet, noting any extra syllables at the end, slurs, pauses, or contractions.

4.   Analyze the text for verbal conceits. (See Part I.)

A sonnet by William Shakespeare can serve as an example:

> When in disgrace with Fortune and men's eyes
> I all alone beweep my outcast state,
> And trouble deaf heaven with my bootless cries,
> And look upon myself and curse my fate,
> Wishing me like to one more rich in hope,
> Featur'd like him, like him with friends posess'd,
> Desiring this man's art, and that man's scope,
> With what I most enjoy contented least;
> Yet in these thoughts myself almost despising,
> Haply I think on thee, and then my state
> (Like to the lark at break of day arising
> From sullen earth sings hymns at heaven's gate,
> > For thy sweet love rememb'red such wealth brings
> > That then I scorn to change my state with kings.

First, note words which receive stress naturally:

> When in **disgrace** with **Fortune** and men's **eyes**
> **I** all **alone beweep** my outcast **state,**
> And **trouble deaf heaven** with my **bootless cries,**
> And **look upon myself** and **curse** my **fate,**
> **Wishing** me **like** to **one** more **rich** in **hope,**
> **Featur'd** like **him,** like **him** with **friends posess'd,**
> **Desiring this** man's **art,** and **that** man's **scope,**
> With **what** I **most enjoy contented least;**
> Yet in these **thoughts myself almost despising,**
> **Haply** I **think** on **thee,** and **then** my **state**
> **(Like** to the **lark** at **break** of **day arising**
> From **sullen earth sings hymns** at heaven's **gate,**
> > For thy sweet **love rememb'red** such **wealth brings**
> > That then I **scorn** to **change** my **state** with **kings.**

☞ 14.   Choose a sonnet by William Shakespeare. Count the number of lines of verse.

☞ 15.   Count the number of syllables in each line of your chosen sonnet by William Shakespeare.

☞ 16. Identify the words in your chosen sonnet which have alternate pronunciations with more or less syllables.

Second, note the simple subject, verb, and object:

> When in disgrace with Fortune and men's eyes
> I all alone BEWEEP MY outcast STATE
> AND TROUBLE deaf HEAVEN with my bootless cries
> AND LOOK UPON MYSELF AND CURSE MY FATE
> Wishing me like to one more rich in hope
> Featur'd like him, like him with friends posess'd
> Desiring this man's art and that man's scope
> With what I most enjoy contented least
> YET in these thoughts myself almost despising
> Haply I THINK ON THEE AND THEN MY STATE
> Like to the lark at break of day arising
> From sullen earth SINGS HYMNS at heaven's gate
>   For thy sweet love rememb'red such wealth brings
>   That then I scorn to change my state with kings.

The single simple sentence version of the sonnet would be:

"I BEWEEP MY STATE AND TROUBLE HEAVEN AND LOOK UPON MYSELF AND CURSE MY FATE, YET I THINK ON THEE AND THEN MY STATE SINGS HYMNS."

☞ 17. Scan your chosen sonnet, noting where stresses fall naturally. Identify the simple subject, verb, and object of each sentence.

Third, find the feet, and any pauses, slurs, contractions, or extra syllables.

```
      x     '    x    '    x     '    x    '   x       '
   [When in] [dis grace] [with For] [tune and] [men's eyes]

      x '   x '    x     '     x    '   x      '
   [I all] [a lone] [BEWEEP] [MY out] [cast STATE]

      x       '         x     '   x     '    x    '   x
   [AND TROUBLE] [deaf HEA] [VEN with] [my boot] [less

      '
   cries]
```

   x   '   x   '   x   '   x   '   x
[AND LOOK] [U PON] [MY SELF] [AND CURSE] [MY
 '
FATE]

 '   x   x   '   x   '   x   '   x   '
[Wish ing] [me like] [to one] [more rich] [in hope]

 '   x   x   '   x   '   x   '   x   '
[Fea tur'd] [like him] [like him] [with friends] [po sess'd]

 x   '   x   '   x   '   x   '   x   '
[De si] [ring this] [man's art] [and that] [man's scope]

 x   '   x   '   x   '   x   '   x   '
[With what] [I most] [en joy] [con ten] [ted least]

 x   '   x   '   x   '   x   '   x   '   x
[YET in] [these thoughts] [my self] [al most] [des pis] [ing]

 '   x   x   '   x   '   x   '   x
[Hap ly] [I THINK] [ON THEE] [AND THEN] [MY
 '
STATE]

 x   '   x   '   x   '   x '   x   '   x
[(Like to] [the lark] [at break] [of day] [a ris] [ing]

 x   '   x   '   x   '   x   '   x   '
[From sul] [len earth] [SINGS HYMNS] [at hea] [ven's gate]

 x   '   x   '   x   '   x   '   x   '
[For thy] [sweet love] [re mem] [b'red such] [wealth brings]

 x   '   x   '   x   '   x   '   x   '
[That then] [I scorn] [to change] [my state] [with kings]

☞ 17. Scan your chosen sonnet to give each syllable either an accent or a non-accent mark.

☞ 18. Divide each line of your chosen sonnet into feet. Note any caesuras. Identify the verse form.

Finally, identify the **verbal conceits** (See Part I):

    [When *in*] [d*i*s grace] [with For] [tune and] [men's *e*yes]
    [*I all*] [a *l*one] [be *weep*] [my ou*t*] [cast *state*]
    [<u>And</u> tr'ble] [d*ea*f h*ea*] [ven with] [my boot][l*ess* cr*ies*]
    [<u>And</u> *l*ook] [u pon] [my *s*elf] [<u>and</u> *c*urse] [my fate]
    [W*i*sh ing] [me like] [to one] [more r*i*ch] [in hope]

[*Fea* tur'd] [*like him*] [*like him*] [with *friends*] [po *sess*'d]
[De *si*] [ring *this*] [*man's* art] [and *that*] [*man's* scope]
[*With what*] [I *most*] [en joy] [con ten] [ted *least*]
[Yet in] [*these thoughts*] [*my self*] [a*l most*] [des p*i*] [*sing*]
[Hap ly] [I *think*] [on thee] [and *then*] [*my* state]
[(*Li*ke to] [the *l*ark] [at br*ea*k] [of d*a*y] [a r*i*s] [ing]
[From sul] [len earth] [*sings* h*ymns*] [at *hea*] [ven's gate]
[For thy] [*sweet* love] [re mem] [*b*'red such] [wealth *b*rings]
[*That then*] [*I* scorn] [to ch*a*nge] [my st*a*te] [with king*s*]

☞　19.　Identify the verbal conceits and rhetorical devices in
　　　　your chosen sonnet.

VARIETY

Playwrights vary metric form for several reasons. First, playwrights
can use meter to communicate pronunciation to the actors. Manipu-
lating the verse form lets the playwright control the actors mouths.
For example, putting two accented syllables together forces an actor
to hesitate between them. Contrariwise, putting two unaccented syllables together encourages the actor to slur them together. Long lines
suggest **elision**. For example, in *Julius Caesar*, Mark Antony declares:

　　x　'　　x　'　x　'　x　'　x　'　　x
　　[I come] [to bur] [y Cae] [sar not] [to praise] [him]

In pronunciation the "him" is slurred into "praise":

　　x　'　　x　'　x　'　x　'　x　'
　　[I come] [to bur] [y Cae] [sar not] [to praise'm]

Likewise, in *The Comedy of Errors*, the Duke probably contracts "she"
with "is," and makes "virtuous" and "reverend" two syllables to make
the line trochaic:

　　She is a vir tu ous and a rev ver end la dy

becomes

<pre>
 '   x   '   x   '   x   '   x   '   x
[She's a] [vir tous] [and a] [rev rend] [la dy]
</pre>

By altering the length of a line, playwrights send messages to actors. Short lines suggest pause. Shortening a line encourages the actor to find silent time in the line to accommodate the missing measures. Sometimes a short line signals to the actor to add a syllable in the pronunciation of a word. For example, the meter of *Humpty Dumpty* requires "Humpty" to have three syllables [Hum-pe-ty] in the first two lines but only two syllables [Hump-ty] in the final line.

Units of thought usually begin at the beginning of a line, and end at the end of a line. This encourages the actor to think of as line as a measure of thought requiring a pause at the end. (A lone accented final syllable usually calls for a **caesura**, a pause or hesitation, at the ends of the line.) When playwrights carry over a sentence, phrase, or thought to next line — **enjambment** — they signal to the actor that a pause or elongation of the line's final word or syllable should mark the formal end of a line, but not the end of the thought. The actor's mind should remain suspended until the sentence, phrase, or thought is completed in the next line. For example, in *The Tempest*, Prospero enjambs one of his most famous lines (Arrow signs help actors note cases of enjambment in their scores.)

<pre>
  '   x   '   x →
These our actors,
x ' x ' x   '   x   ' x '
As I fortold you, were all spirits, and
x   '   x ' x '   x   '   →
Are melted into air, thin air;
</pre>

Likewise in *Othello*, Iago's enjambs his planning:

<pre>
  '   x   x   '   x   ' x   ' x '   x
Dang'rous conceits are in their natures poisons,
   x   ' x ' x   '   x   ' x '
Which at the first are scarce found to distaste,
   x   '   x ' x   ' x '   x '
But, with a little act upon the blood,
</pre>

    x   ˈ   x   ˈ   x   ˈ   x
Burn like the mines of sulphur.

(Notice again how scansion reveals the possibility of alternative pronunciations.)

Another passage from Shakespeare's *Othello* shows how metric variety communicates possibilities to an actor.

> OTHELLO: Whip me ye devils,
> From the possession of this heavenly sight!
> Blow me about in winds! roast me in sulpher!

The first line has but five syllables. Shakespeare thus gives the actor five beats of silence with which to play either before or after the words of the first line. With the second and third lines, the playwright's verse offers additional insight into playing both elisions and a dynamic pause:

    ˈ   x   x ˈ x
[Whip me] [ye de] [vils] _ _ _ _ _

or

          ˈ   x   x ˈ   x
_ _ _ _ _ [Whip me] [ye de] [vils]
  ˈ   x   x ˈ   x ˈ   x ˈ   x ˈ
[From the] [po ses] [sion of] [this hea'n] [ly sight]
  ˈ   x   ˈ   x ˈ   x ˈ   x ˈ   x
[Blow mea] [bout in] [winds _][roast me'n] [sul pher]

Third, playwrights choose individual speech sounds and devices to heighten a character's diction which, in turn, give the verse variety. Repeated vowel and consonant sounds give musculature to the spoken verse. A clear understanding of why particular words, phrases, vocal conceits, and rhetorical devices are chosen by your particular character at a particular moment in a particular situation will give motivational nuance to the verse. Consideration of all of the techniques will give your utterance, of even the most familiar piece of stage verse, a unique performance rhythm.

FIGURES
AND TROPES

In the Renaissance, imagery was known as "figures" or "tropes," from the Greek word for "turns." School children in Shakespeare's England were expected to know all rhetorical devices by name. Consequently, in playing on stage "figures were 'made manifest' by the intonation and stress which showed the relation in which the words stand to one another both as sound and as sense."[21]

Basic to all figures and tropes are the techniques of heightened diction discussed in Part I. Repetition and antithesis were key architectural devices upon which to build elaborate word structures. In the Renaissance, metaphors, similes, and allegories were very well-known modes of expression among educated and artistic people. With each figure, one thing is said while something else is meant; word usage departs from the normal to create new expressions. Bert Joseph notes that a "figure of words is in essence a pattern of sound; the pattern need not be used to enforce the sense, but in most cases, especially with Shakespeare, meaning and emotion are bound up in the structure of the pattern."[22]

With figures and tropes, language is used in, or aspires to attain, a metaphorical sense. The thing said has been called either the "analogue" or the "vehicle." The thing meant has been called either the "subject" or the "tenor." Scholars have reduced the number of figures to seven:

Synecdoche — describes by substituting a part (analogue/vehicle) for the whole (subject/tenor), as with "He was the King's legs" rather than "He was the King's messenger." Legs are a part (vehicle) of the whole messenger (tenor).

Metonymy — from the Greek for "change of name," describes by substituting a word related to subject for the subject word itself. For example, with "Friends, Romans, and countrymen, lend me your ears...," "ears" is the analogue/vehicle for attention, the subject/tenor.

Simile — describes by explicitly comparing the subject/tenor with the analogue/vehicle, and links the comparison with either the word "like" or the word "as." Hamlet instructs Ophelia with a series of similes: "Be thou as chaste as ice, as pure as snow...."

Metaphor — from the Greek for "transfer or carry across," describes by directly comparing the subject/tenor with the analogue/vehicle, and does not use "like" or "as." Macbeth coins a metaphor with "Life's but a walking shadow...."

Personification — gives human characteristics or traits to non-human abstractions, animals, or objects. Hamlet's friend Horatio chooses a personification with "The morn in russet mantle clad, walks..."

Symbol — from the Greek "to compare," makes a word, phrase, or image represent something else. For example, Psalm 23 makes the image of a shepherd represent the Lord.

Allegory — a system of symbols in narrative form. For example, Psalm 23's narration of the relationship between the shepherd and his sheep, represents the relationship between God and the human narrator.

Verse often uses figures and tropes in a complex manner. So organic are the figures and tropes employed to the intentions of the character, that Bert Joseph believes "if we approach a passage of Shakespeare primarily by way of systematic analysis into the individual rhetorical figures, we shall find that it leads to a complete imaginative realizing of his meaning."[23]

☞ 20. Identify all figures and tropes of speech in a nursery rhyme or *Jabberwocky*. Underline or color the important words in each figure. Speak the rhyme as if diagramming with your voice the relationship of one rhetorical figure to another.

☞ 21. Identify all figures and tropes of speech in a sonnet. Underline or color the important words in each figure. Speak the sonnet as if diagramming with your voice the relationship of one speech sound (consonant and vowel) to another.

☞ 22. Identify all figures and tropes of speech in a monologue. Underline or color the important words in each figure. Speak the monologue as if diagramming with your voice the relationship of one rhetorical figure to another.

IMAGERY

Imagery is the conjuration of pictorial appeals to the senses. In the Hebrew Testament of the Bible, human beings are conceived as images — mental sensory imitations — of God. Similarly, poets of the stage create by making images. In *Shakespeare's Metrical Art*, George T. Wright points out that "the complex figurative language Shakespeare uses — especially his strong imagery — continually magnifies the intensity and emphasis with which his characters' words must be spoken." Psychologists have identified seven kinds of mental images:

Visual: sight (brightness, clarity, color, motion).

Auditory: hearing.

Olfactory: smell.

Gustatory: taste.

Tactile: touch (temperature, texture).

Organic: awareness of heartbeat, pulse, breathing, digestion.

Kinesthetic: awareness of muscle tension and movement.

Humpty Dumpty contains mostly visual images: Humpty himself, the wall, the horses and men. In addition, an actor could imagine hearing Humpty sit and fall down, as well as the sounds of the horses and men as they worked to put him together. Perhaps Humpty, the horses, and the men had distinct odors.

☞ 23. Identify the sensory images in your nursery rhyme or *Jabberwocky*. Color each type of sense image with a different color pencil, crayon, or marker.

☞ 24. Speak the nursery rhyme or *Jabberwocky* employing the technique of **substitution** introduced in Part I. Before saying the words describing each image, pause to recollect in great detail a particular image from your own life analogous to that being described. Take as long as possible. Place each image somewhere around you, **as if** you were there, now, amid the actual objects. Don't pretend anything. Listen until you hear. Touch until you feel. Look until you see. Wait until you sense it, before you say it.

Shakespeare's Sonnet 29, our study sonnet, begins with the speaker weeping, an image involving all seven of the senses. Troubling deaf heaven with "bootless cries" involves the auditory, organic, and kinesthetic senses. "And look upon myself" begins a series of visual sensations, culminating in the visual thinking on "thee" which produces the kinesthetic and organic sensations associated with happiness. The image of the "lark at break of day" involves seeing, hearing, and perhaps smelling and touching. "Sweet love" involves taste, while "scorn" can involve organic and kinesthetic senses.

☞ 25. Identify the sensory images in your sonnet. Color each type of sense image with a different color pencil, crayon, or marker.

☞ 26. Speak the sonnet employing the technique of **substitution** introduced in Part I. Before saying the words describing each image, pause to recollect in great detail a particular image from your own life analogous to that being described. Take as long as possible. Place each image somewhere around you, **as if** you were there, now, amid the actual objects. Don't pretend anything. Listen until you hear. Touch until you feel. Look until you see. Wait until you sense it, before you say it.

☞ 27. Identify the sensory images in your verse monologue. Color each type of sense image with a different color pencil, crayon, or marker.

☞ 28. Speak the verse monologue employing the technique of **substitution** introduced in Part I. Before saying the words describing each image, pause to recollect in great detail a particular image from your own life analogous to that being described. Take as long as possible. Place each image somewhere around you, **as if** you were there, now, amid the actual objects. Don't pretend anything. Listen until you hear. Touch until you feel. Look until you see. Wait until you sense it, before you say it.

SPEAKING VERSE

Verse is not spoken by "hitting" each accent like a metronome. Nor is verse spoken simply by "punching" the natural stresses, by increasing volume or intensity. (Some actors prefer to think of stress as lengthening the duration of the accented syllable's vowel sound.) Spoken verse is a dynamic balance between two related, but competing, demands. Like Goldilocks, verse demands neither too slavish a following to metrical sing-song, nor too informal a disregard of the needs of the metrical context. Effective verse speaking preserves the meter and line, but so covertly and flexibly as to create the illusion of believable speech.

Actors need to master the verse's imagery, figures and tropes, heightened diction, and meter to make them deliberate character choices rather than unfortunate necessary evils of performance. As Humpty Dumpty tells Alice in Lewis Carroll's *Through the Looking Glass*:

> "When I use a word," Humpty Dumpty said, in a rather scornful tone, "it means just what I choose it to mean — neither more nor less."
>
> "The question is," said Alice, "whether you can make words mean so many different things."
>
> "The question is," said Humpty Dumpty, "which is to be the master — that's all."

☞ 29. Paraphrase and speak the nursery rhyme or *Jabberwocky*. Learn it thought by thought, rather than word by word. Figure out how one thought could lead to the next.

☞ 30. Speak the nursery rhyme or *Jabberwocky*, stressing only the simple subject, verb and object. Hurry through the rest of the words. As Dame Edith Evans (1888–1976) noted:

You learn to go from emphatic word to emphatic word like springboards, and when you want to slow up you lean on them a bit. Once you know about that, it's ordinary talk really, it's life, it's the way we talk. After all, we don't emphasize every word when we talk do we?[24]

☞ 31.   Verse moves through a series of discoveries made by the speaker. Each discovery prompts the speaker to say more. Insert "like" or "I mean' before each new discovery in your nursery rhyme or *Jabberwocky*.

☞ 32.   Paraphrase and speak the sonnet. Learn it thought by thought, rather than word by word. Figure out how one thought could lead to the next.

☞ 33.   Speak the sonnet, stressing only the simple subjects, verbs and objects in each sentence. Hurry through the rest of the words.

☞ 34.   Insert "like" or "I mean' before each new discovery in your sonnet.

When in, like, disgrace with, like, Fortune and, like, men's eyes
I, I mean, all alone, like, beweep my, like, outcast state,
And, like, trouble deaf heaven with my, like, bootless cries,
And, I mean, look upon myself and, like, curse my fate,
I mean, Wishing me like to one, like, more rich in, like, hope,
I mean, Featur'd like him, I mean, like him with friends, like, posess'd,
Like, Desiring this man's, like, art, and that man's, like, scope,
I mean, With what I most enjoy, like, contented least;
Yet, like, in these thoughts, I mean, myself, like, almost despising,
I mean, Haply I, like, think on thee, and, like, then my, like, state
I mean, (Like to the lark, like, at break of day, like, arising
From, like, sullen earth, I mean, sings, like, hymns at, like, heaven's gate,
*   I mean, For thy sweet love, like, rememb'red, like, such wealth, like, brings*
*   Like, That then I, like, scorn to, like, change my, like, state with, like, kings.*

Speak the sonnet, then speak the sonnet without the

"likes" and "I mean" but using your voice to note the discoveries.

☞ 35. Paraphrase and speak the verse monologue. Learn it thought by thought, rather than word by word. Figure out how one thought could lead to the next.

☞ 36. Speak the verse monologue, stressing only the simple subjects, verbs and objects in each sentence. Hurry through the rest of the words.

☞ 37. Insert "like" or "I mean' before each new discovery in your verse monologue. Speak the monologue, then speak it without the "likes" and "I mean" but using your voice to note the discoveries.

☞ 38. Speak the nursery rhyme or *Jabberwocky* to a metronome. Let each metrical accent fall on a tick. Pause in rhythm, too. Increase the rate and speak the nursery rhyme. Decrease the rate and speak the nursery rhyme.

☞ 39. Speak the sonnet to a metronome. Let each metrical accent fall on a tick. Pause in rhythm, too. Increase the rate and speak the sonnet. Decrease the rate and speak the sonnet.

☞ 40. Speak the verse monologue to a metronome. Let each metrical accent fall on a tick. Pause in rhythm, too. Increase the rate and speak the verse monologue. Decrease the rate and speak the verse monologue.

☞ 41. Speak the nursery rhyme or *Jabberwocky*, balancing the verse's meter with your natural diction impulses to create the illusion of believable speech.

☞ 42. Repeat the previous exercise with your sonnet.

☞ 43. Repeat the previous exercise with your verse monologue.

VERSE DIALOGUE

With dialogue, the playwright's verse can give insights into timing between characters. For example, a scene between Desdemona and Othello in Shakespeare's play can benefit from actors' scansion:

> **DESDEMONA:** Pray you let Cassio be receiv'd again.
>
> **OTHELLO:** Fetch me the handkerchief, my mind mis-
> gives.
>
> **DESDEMONA:** Come, come;
> You'll never meet a more sufficient man.
>
> **OTHELLO:** The handkerchief!
>
> **DESDEMONA:**   I pray talk me of Cassio.
>
> **OTHELLO:** The handkerchief!
>
> **DESDEMONA:**   A man that all his time
> Hath found his good fortunes on your love.
> Shar'd dangers with you —
>
> **OTHELLO:** The handkerchief!
>
> **DESDEMONA:** I'faith, you are to blame.
>
> **OTHELLO:** 'Zounds!

After locating the natural stresses, place the syllables in feet:

Des: [Pray you] [let Cas] [syo be] [re ceiv'd] [a gain]

Oth: [Fetch me] [the hand] [ker chief] [my mind] [mis gives]

Des: [Come come][_ _][_ _][_ _][_ _]

or

```
         x '   x ' x ' x '    x        '
Des: [_ _][_ _][_ _][_ _] [Come come]
```

or

```
         x '     x      '   x ' x ' x '
Des: [_ _] [Come come][_ _][_ _][_ _]
```

or

```
         x '   x '    x      '   x ' x '
Des: [_ _] [_ _][Come come][_ _][_ _]
```

or

```
         x '   x ' x '    x     '   x '
Des: [_ _] [_ _][_ _][Come come][_ _]
```

or

```
     x            '                          x    '
[Come come] overlaps Othello's [mis gives]
     x     '   x    '   x   '    x '    x         '
[You'll ne] [ver meet] [a more] [suf fi] [cient man]
                 x    '     x      '   x ' x ' x '
Othello: [The hand] [ker chief][_ _][_ _][_ _]
```

or

```
 x '     x      '     x      '   x ' x '
[_ _][The hand] [ker chief][_ _][_ _]
```

or

```
 x ' x '    x      '     x      '   x '
[_ _][_ _][The hand] [ker chief][_ _]
```

or

```
 x ' x ' x '    x      '     x      '
[_ _][_ _][_ _][The hand] [ker chief]
```

or

    x   '   x   '
[The hand] [ker chief] could overlap Desdemona's

  x ' x   '   x   '
[suf fi] {cient man], or Othello's [The hand] could merely

              x   '
overlap Desdemona's [cient man].

If the actor playing Othello chooses the first reading, then Desdemona's next speech completes the metric line, if she overlaps her [I pray] with Othello's final syllables [ker chief]:

                       x '   '   x x ' x '
Desdemona: [I pray] [talk me] [of Cas] [si o]

           x   '   x   '
Othello: [The hand] [ker chief]

And Desdemona completes the line with

                       x '   x '   x '
Desdemona: [A man] [that all] [his time]

  x   '   x   '   x   '   x   '
[Hath foundis] [good for] [tunes on] [your love]

  x   '   x   '   x '
[Shar'd dan] [gers with] [you _]

Desdemona may stop herself for a beat before Othello speaks and completes the line.

           x   '   x   '
Othello: [The hand] [ker chief]

Desdemona then completes Othello's line in turn.

                x '   x   '   x '
Desdemona: [I' faith] [you are] [to blame]

Othello can wait nine beats before his "'Zounds!" or overlap Desdemona's "blame" with the exit oath.

Playwrights can spread the ten syllables of a line of blank verse among several characters. In *The Alchemist*, Ben Jonson divides a line of epithets among Subtle, his housekeeper Face, and their friend Dol Common:

Face: Bawd!
Sub: Cowherd!
Face: Conjurer!
Sub: Cutpurse!
Face: Witch!
Dol: Oh me!

☞ 44. Sit facing another actor and begin the "What a Day!" Exercise from Part I. The other actor should repeat as the Repetition Exercise begins. After a while, slide into the paraphrase of the nursery rhyme in whatever mood or attitude your recollection has produced. After a while, slide into the actual nursery rhyme in whatever mood or attitude you are in. Your goal should be balance your spontaneous speech inclinations with the metered verse text, without altering the memorized text.

☞ 45. Repeat the previous exercise with your sonnet.

☞ 46. Repeat the previous exercise with your verse monologue.

☞ 47. Repeat Exercise 44, this time with both actors recalling things from their day, sliding into paraphrases, then into nursery rhymes, and repeating. Seek to connect your recollections and nursery rhyme to what you are hearing from your partner.

☞ 45. Repeat the previous exercise with your sonnet.

☞ 46. Repeat the previous exercise with your verse monologue.

☞ 47. Repeat Exercise 44, using only the nursery rhymes or *Jabberwocky*.

☞ 48. Repeat the previous exercise, using only the sonnets.

☞ 49. Repeat the previous exercise, using only the verse monologues.

☞ 50. Memorize the lines for a character in Open Scene 1-E or 2-E (found in Appendix 2) AS IF a monologue. (These are Elizabethan "translations" of the Open Scenes you performed in Part I.) As in Part I, perform the Open Scene with a partner, after filling with a strong emotion, repeating until something happens to make you go on, and while engaged in a commonplace activity.

☞ 51. Play the Open Scene again, but this time repeating silently. Wait until something happens to make you go on, but realize that **nothing** can be, and often is, "something" to perceive to makes you go on. Also, "something" can happen to make you go on in the middle of the other actor's line; you do not need to be polite by waiting until the other actor is finished. Say your line when you must, even if it interrupts or overlaps the other actor. For example, B might feel like saying "Truly," after hearing only the words "Thou can'st." If so, B can either say the words, or begin to say the words, but "tread water" with silent repetitions of "Truly," until A finishes with the words "mean so."

☞ 52. Repeat the previous exercise, with both actors engaged in a joint activity.

☞ 53. Choose one of the blank verse looped pairs in Appendix 5. Analyze the **heightened diction** and acknowledge it, choose it, "coin it," in your speaking. With a partner, play the loop as a seamless scene: A begins. B repeats A's line and the repetition continues until something happens to make B say B's line. A then repeats B's line and the repetition continues until something happens to make A say A's line again. B then repeats A's line and the scene goes on endlessly. The goal is to listen and respond honestly and spontaneously, while acknowledging and choosing to employ heightened diction.

☞ 54. Choose a verse scene. Analyze the verse individually, and then with your partner. Paraphrase the lines and read your lines as a prose monologue. Then read the lines of your character as a verse monologue. Note when intentions seem to change. Play the first unit of action with the other actor in the scene in your paraphrase, repeating each expression until something happens to make you go on. Gradually add the verse language while retaining the repetition. Say "I don't believe you" if you are not convinced by what your partner says.

☞ 55. With the other actor, play the first four lines of your first unit of action as a Repetition Exercise. Wait for something to happen before going on. At the end of the four lines, return to the first line, AS IF in an endless loop. Continue with the scene, adding one line at a time to the Repetition Exercise.

☞ 56. Play the entire scene to a metronome, keeping each accented syllable on a tick. Vary the rate of the metronome and repeat the scene. This exercise implants the beat in your subconscious, so that as you ease the meter in actual performance, the rhythmic pulse will continue

☞ 57. Analyze your character according to the checklist of
questions in Appendix 3. Use the information gained
in playing the scene.

POETIC CHARACTER

When playing characters who choose to speak in verse, actors need to
go beyond the analysis done for characters who speak only prose. Certainly in everyday life you would need to be a certain type of person,
or have a certain goal, or be in a special relationship, or find yourself
in a particular situation to choose to speak in verse. The same is true
for characters on stage.

When your character speaks verse, ask many questions.

✔ Why does my character choose to speak verse in this particular situation?

✔ What does my character hope to achieve though the use of verse?

✔ What impression does my character hope to create?

✔ How does the verse further that impression?

✔ What emotion does my character wish to generate in the people in
the circumstance?

✔ How does the verse help?

Within a scene, particular verbal choices should be analyzed.

✔ Why does my character choose these particular words, figures,
tropes, or images in this particular situation?

✔ What does my character hope to achieve though the use of these
particular words, figures, tropes, or images?

✔ What impression does my character hope to create?

✔ How do these particular words, figures, tropes, or images further that impression?

✔ What emotion does my character wish to generate in the people in the circumstance?

✔ How do these particular words, figures, tropes, or images help?

VARIATION TWO:

PLAYING COMEDY

THE NATURE OF HUMOR

When babies are only five weeks old, they begin to laugh. Why? The reflex seems to have no apparent biological purpose. Few, if any, other living things contort their faces and make such sounds. Tickling and peek-a-boo are the forerunners of what adults call humor. Human beings are unique in the ability to create and appreciate humor. The French playwright and philosopher Voltaire (1694–1778) believed God to be a comedian playing to an audience afraid to laugh! Why afraid? Perhaps because, as the English novelist George Eliot (1819–80) observed in *Daniel Deronda* (1874), "a difference in taste in jokes is a great strain on the affections." But the question remains: Why humor?

The German philosopher Friedrich Nietzsche (1844–1900) thought laughter a conscious response to human beings' unique recognition of their mortality — "Man alone suffers so excruciatingly in the world that he was compelled to invent laughter." Some sociologists suggest that laughter may have arisen as a vocal sign among early human beings to signal the end of danger.[25] Some psycho-biologists propose that laughter may have arisen as a sign that something useful had suddenly and surprisingly been discovered or gained. Psychologist Lev S. Vygotsky (1896–1934) believed laughter to be a reflex triggered by abstract or symbolic information about either the satisfaction of lusty desires or the victory over conflict.[26] The essayist Norman Cousins' (1915–90) experiments with laughter as a healing technique suggest that laughter may release endorphins, brain hormones which reduce the sensation of pain and affect the emotions. The British writer Doris Lessing (1919–) maintains that "laughter is by definition healthy."

Psychologists and psychiatrists have even sought to create a personality profile for a comedian or humorous person. Their studies suggest that professional comedians 1) have a greater than average "sense of boundary security"; 2) come from less than average nurturing mothers (though comedians consider their mothers to have been the opposite); and 3) were "class clowns" as a result of having been picked on or misunderstood as children.[27] "The successful professional comedian is often of above average intelligence, is adept at verbal manipulation and highlighting incongruities, is sensitive to [the] audience and [its] needs and recognizes the basic desire by [the] audience to 'let themselves go' and laugh, with the aim to escaping from their everyday pedestrian mode of functioning and reasoning, and deriving pleasure from this semi-voluntary regression. [The professional comedian] may develop [a] talent for the comic in response to early pressures to cope with distress by being funny either in the family or at schools and having discovered [a] talent for making others laugh, develops this further into a profession."[28]

Until relatively recently, few women were comics. In 1957 the English comedian Anna Russell (1911–) suggested "the reason that there are so few women comics is that so few women can bear being laughed at." With the women's movement, self-esteem and power have entered more women's lives. As Rita Mae Brown (1944–) notes, "Humor comes from self-confidence. There's an aggressive element to it." Today, women comics are not yet as common as male comics.

By now you probably agree with the American humorist Robert Benchley's (1889–1945) observation that defining and analyzing comedy is the pastime of humorless people. But even comedians have succumbed to the lure. Early in this century, the American showman George M. Cohan (1878–1942) listed "some things men laugh at" in *Mclure's Magazine*:

1. "Giving a man a resounding whack on the back under the guise of friendship."

2. "A man gives a woman a whack on the back, believing in an absent-minded moment that the woman (to whom he is talking) is a man."

3. "One character steps on the sore foot of another character, causing the latter to jump with pain."

4. "The spectacle of a man laden with many large bundles."

5. "A man or a woman starts to lean his or her elbow on a table or arm of a chair, the elbow slipping off abruptly and suddenly precipitating him or her forward."

6. "One character imitating the walk of another character, who is walking in front of him and can not see him."

7. "A man consuming a drink of considerable size at one quick gulp."

8. "A character who, on entering an interior or room scene, stumbles over a rug."

9. "Intoxication in almost any form."

10. "Two men in heated conversation. One starts to leave. Suddenly, as if fearing the other will kick him while his back is turned, this man bends his body inward (as if he actually had been kicked) and sidles off."

11. "A man who, in trying to light his cigar or cigarette, strikes match after match in an attempt to keep one lighted."

12. "The use of a swear word."

13. "A man proclaims his defiance of his wife while the latter is presumably out of hearing. As the man is speaking, his wife's voice is heard calling him. Meekly he turns and goes to her."

14. "A pair of lovers who try several times to kiss, and each time are

interrupted by the entrance of someone or by the ringing of the doorbell or telephone-bell or something of the sort."

15. "A bashful man and a not bashful woman are seated on a bench or divan. As the woman gradually edges up to the man, the man just as gradually edges away from her."

Mr. Cohan concludes by observing that "a painful situation apparently contains elements of the ridiculous so long as the pain is not actually of a serious nature . . . The most successful tricks or jokes are all based on the idea of pain or embarrassment." Long ago the Greek philosopher Aristotle (c. 384–c. 322 B.C.E.) came to the same conclusion: "The pleasure of comedy is associated with the perception of a defect or ugliness that is neither painful nor injurious. It is associated with our sense of disproportion."[29]

Cohan is unique neither in his attempt to identify the nature of comedy nor in his conclusions. Indeed, from the beginning of written analysis, literary critics and comic performers have tried to locate the source of laughter. Unfortunately for actors, most attempts have considered the comic "mood," "spirit," "form," or "idea," and usually have focused on the comic writer. Few, if any, attempts have been made to explain to the would-be actors of comic characters the peculiar approach they will need to take.

INCONGRUITY AND IGNORANCE

All discussions of comedy eventually arrive at the idea of "incongruity." Humor itself has been defined as the ability to perceive relationships between people, objects, or ideas in an incongruous way. People with a "sense of humor" not only have this perception, but also can communicate this perception to others and understand and enjoy others' communication of the perception.

Incongruity involves two perspectives, two lines of probability. The philosopher Arthur Schopenhauer (1788–1860) noted that "the cause of laughter in every case is simply the sudden perception of the incongruity between a concept and the real objects which have been thought through it in some relation."[30] Humor, laughter, and comedy arise from either the juxtaposition of two different perspectives or the collision of two distinct lines of probability. "Why did the moron take a yardstick to bed? To see how long he slept." One perspective or probability—yardsticks measure length of space—collides with another—the word "length" can mean either space or time. The moron is laughable because he is unaware of the existence of an alternative perspective to the one he has regarding "length." As Samuel Kahn (1897–1981) noted, "the comic character lacks insight and is ignorant of himself. The comic character is invisible to himself but visible to all the world. Such stupidity is quite laughable."[31]

Comic characters seem to live in what quantum physicists would call a "parallel universe" which, when it collides with either that of the audience or of another character, produces laughter. In the right hemisphere of the observer's brain two divergent meanings are simultaneously and rapidly presented. When the brain resolves the incongruous lines, the *gestalt* is reordered; in other words, the observer's conceptual framework is reorganized to allow for the new, previously incongruous, information. This happens when an audience laughs. It rarely happens in a comic character.

In fact, most effective comic characters possess an ignorance of an alternate perspective or line of probability. For example, Cohan's first illustration can be funny only if the backslapping character is unaware that he is hurting the other character. It is even more humorous if the character in pain tries to keep the backslapper ignorant of the other perspective — his pain. Cohan's second example also depends upon ignorance. Number 13 requires the husband's ignorance of his wife's proximity. *Humor increases with the characters' confidence that their own perception is not only the correct perspective, but the only perspective.* In fact, if characters thought they were in a funny situation, the audience would not be amused. As the great silent film comedian Buster Keaton

(1895–1966) noted, "One of the first things I noticed was that whenever I smiled or let the audience suspect how much I was enjoying myself they didn't seem to laugh as much as usual."[32]

Number 3 depends upon the character's ignorance either that the foot is sore or that "innocent" contact could cause great pain. Cohan's number 14 depends upon the lovers' conviction that each interruption they deal with will be the last interruption. The more convinced the lovers are that no further interruptions are possible, the funnier the next interruption is.

The French theorist Henri Bergson (1859–1941) wrote that "a comic character is generally comic in proportion to his ignorance of himself." A comic character is also comic in proportion to how convinced she is that she is *not* ignorant at all. But if comedy needs ignorance, it also needs awareness. The great American comedian Bert Lahr (1895–1967) observed, "You can do almost anything on stage if you do it as if you haven't the slightest idea there's something wrong with what you're doing."[33] Falling on a rug or slipping off a chair's arm are humorous because the character was unaware of something which the audience knows. Consequently, *actors need to take the audience's perspective into account when analyzing, creating, and performing comic characters.*

For a character to be seen as ignorant of an impending incongruity, an audience must be aware of the alternative perspective. Drunkenness is only funny if the intoxicated characters believe that they are perfectly sober; they must believe that their perspective is the correct and logical one. They can understand neither why some normally easy actions are now difficult to do, nor why other previously difficult things are now quite easy to do. The answer, for comic drunks, always lies outside of themselves.

The misperception of reality is often the basis of comedy. When a character holds a perspective at odds with the one held by the audience, laughter results. For example, number 7 is humorous because the audience misperceives the man's capacity to drink in one gulp. Number 10 is laughable because the man perceives a kick when none was inflicted. Likewise, Cohan's number 6 can be funny in two instances: 1) the person walking doesn't realize what the imitator knows — that his or her walk is abnormal, or 2) the person walking has a normal walk from the audience's perspective, but the imitator is under the false impression that the walk is laughable. Both instances require two perspectives — the "normal" one of the audience and the mistaken one of a character. Impersonators and burlesques of familiar stories are humorous because the two perspectives exist at one time in one person. For example, Dana Carvey's (1955–) impersonation of George Bush lets the audience see both the president's perspective of himself and the actor's perspective of the president in one performance.

UPHOLDING "THE NORMAL"

In some tribal societies, clowns could make the group laugh by pretending to drink cow urine and enjoy the taste. Violating a social taboo is a common technique for generating laughter in a cohesive community. Every community, every audience, is unique, and every audience has a perspective and a scheme of probability based upon what it considers "normal," "logical," "acceptable," or "tasteful." Comedy is relative to a group's experience. As comedian Johnny Carson (1925–) observed, "Everything is relative in comedy. Tragedy, no. If you see a serious play, everybody that sees that serious play will come out with almost the same reaction. If something's sad, it's sad . . . But when you walk out and do a piece of humorous business, it's not going to affect everybody the same because it is all relative to their own individual experience with it — how they relate to it."[34] Comedian Dick Gregory (1932–) concurs, saying that black people have a different sense of humor from white people "because the Negro has a different set of values from the white man."[35]

Neo-Classical critics insisted that comedy serves the social function of upholding community "values" by ridiculing individual abnormality, unacceptability, tastelessness, and indecency. The English critic John Dennis (1657–1734) wrote that "the design of Comedy is to amend the follies of Mankind, by exposing them." The English philosopher Thomas Hobbes (1588–1679) believed that humor was the "sudden glory arising from some sudden conception of some eminency in ourselves; by comparison with the infirmity of others or with our own formerly."

Humor may reinforce a group's normative standard and discourage deviance from that standard. Among, and within, groups, humor is hierarchical. Directed downward, humor can either reinforce and justify the possession of power or act as a tool to acquire additional power. Directed upward (in the absence of superiors), humor attacks the hierarchy through ridicule. The powerless vent their frustrations against the those who do not deserve their disproportionate amount of power.

COMIC POWER PLAYING

The actress Uta Hagen (1919–) observed that "in almost all human relationships — or at least in certain areas of a relationship — one person dominates and the other submits; one person leads and the other follows."[36] Comic characters may misperceive their position of power, or assume a manner incongruous for a person with their amount of power. When "The Honeymooners'" Ralph Kramden seeks to get Alice to do something she doesn't want to do, a power play occurs. Powerful people usually remind their partners of their dependent position, threaten to end the relationship, or use physical force. An exasperated Ralph usually is forced to threaten to use his power by sending Alice "to the moon." But, since a comic power play involves misperception or incongruity, Ralph misperceives both his own ability to use physical power and the power distribution in his relationship with Alice. Molière's (1622–73) powerless servant, Sganarelle, on the other hand, always seems to prevail over his master by using the tactics of the powerless — arousal of guilt, retaliation, and wasting his master's time.

☞ 1. Watch comedies on film and television with attention on one character trying to get another character to do something she or he doesn't want to do. Note the tactics of the powerful and the tactics of the powerless.

SUPERIORITY AND COMEDY

The audience knows what the comic character doesn't. The audience sees both lines of probability, while the comic character sees only one. This gives the audience an automatic sense of superiority. Aristotle observed that comic characters are in some way "inferior."[37] Their sense of superiority may also arise from the audience's perception of an a-normality. Psychological studies have shown that the frequency of laughter increases in direct proportion to the size of the audience. Consequently, a group of people might laugh at a retarded person, while any member of that group would probably not laugh if alone. The French writer Honoré de Balzac (1799–1850) thought laughter decreased with age: "As children only do we laugh, and as we travel onward laughter sinks down and dies out like the light of the oil lamp."

Because comedy violates the idea of normalcy, Cohan could expect laughter at example number 12; swearing was less normal, less acceptable, than it is now. *Actors playing comedy need to understand their particular audience's idea of what is "normal."* As the English actor Louis Calvert (1859–1923) wrote, "whereas in tragedy it is often well to ignore the audience so far as possible, in comedy the actor must take his audience into partnership. He must always be conscious of them, and of their changing moods. He has to lead them at times and give rein at others."[38] The spectacle of a man laden with many bundles, number 4, can be funny either if the man has much less trouble than a normal person would, or if he has much more trouble than a normal person would.

Certain themes of abnormality seem to recur. Psychologist Gerald W. Grumet identified the ten most frequent psychodynamic themes in comedy:

1. Aggression.

2. Misfortune, e.g., physical injury.

3. Ineptitude, e.g., stupidity.

4. Family conflict.

5. Social unacceptability, e.g., ugliness.

6. Interpersonal estrangement, e.g. racial or ethnic differences.

7. Criminal behavior or untruthfulness.

8. Sexuality.

9. Money or property.

10. Orality.

The moron joke employs themes #3 Ineptitude and #9 Property (the ruler). Cohan's list of fifteen break down as follows:

1. "Giving a man a resounding whack on the back under the guise of friendship." [#1 Aggression, #2 Misfortune, e.g., physical injury, #3 Ineptitude, e.g., stupidity]

2. "A man gives a woman a whack on the back, believing in an absent-minded moment that the woman (to whom he is talking) is a man." [#1 Aggression, #2 Misfortune, e.g., physical injury, #3 Ineptitude, e.g., stupidity]

3. "One character steps on the sore foot of another character, causing the latter to jump with pain." [#1 Aggression, #2 Misfortune, e.g., physical injury, #3 Ineptitude, e.g., stupidity]

4. "The spectacle of a man laden with many large bundles." [#2 Misfortune, e.g., physical injury, #3 Ineptitude, e.g., stupidity. #9 Money or property]

5. "A man or a woman starts to lean his or her elbow on a table or arm of a chair, the elbow slipping off abruptly and suddenly precipitating him or her forward." [#2 Misfortune, e.g., physical injury, #3 Ineptitude, e.g., stupidity]

6. "One character imitating the walk of another character, who is walking in front of him and can not see him." [#1 Aggression, #3 Ineptitude, e.g., stupidity]

7. "A man consuming a drink of considerable size at one quick gulp." [#3 Ineptitude, e.g., stupidity, #5 Social unacceptability, e.g., ugliness, #10 Orality]

8. "A character who, on entering an interior or room scene, stumbles over a rug." [#2 Misfortune, e.g., physical injury]

9. "Intoxication in almost any form." [#1 Aggression, #2 Misfortune, e.g., physical injury, #3, Ineptitude, e.g., stupidity, #4 Family conflict, #5 Social unacceptability, e.g., ugliness, #6 Interpersonal estrangement, e.g. racial or ethnic differences, #7 Criminal behavior or untruthfulness, #8 Sexuality, #9 Money or property, #10 Orality]

10. "Two men in heated conversation. One starts to leave. Suddenly, as if fearing the other will kick him while his back is turned, this man bends his body inward (as if he actually had been kicked) and sidles off." [#1 Aggression, #2 Misfortune, e.g., physical injury, #3 Ineptitude, e.g., stupidity]

11. "A man who, in trying to light his cigar or cigarette, strikes match after match in an attempt to keep one lighted." [#2 Misfortune, e.g., physical injury, #3 Ineptitude, e.g., stupidity, #9 Money or property]

12. "The use of a swear word." [#1 Aggression, #5 Social unacceptability, e.g., ugliness]

13. "A man proclaims his defiance of his wife while the latter is presumably out of hearing. As the man is speaking, his wife's voice is heard calling him. Meekly he turns and goes to her." [#1 Aggression, #2 Misfortune, e.g., physical injury, #3 Ineptitude, e.g., stupidity, #4 Family conflict]

14. "A pair of lovers who try several times to kiss, and each time are interrupted by the entrance of some one or by the ringing of the doorbell or telephone-bell or something of the sort." [#2 Misfortune, e.g., physical injury, #8 Sexuality]

15. "A bashful man and a not bashful woman are seated on a bench or divan. As the woman gradually edges up to the man, the man just as gradually edges away from her." [#1 Aggression, #3 Ineptitude, e.g., stupidity, #5 Social unacceptability, e.g., ugliness, #8 Sexuality]

SITUATION COMEDY

As we have noted, having difficulty with things can be a source of comedy. When reviewing the circumstances in which comic characters find themselves, you should seek or invent difficulties for your character. In this way, you can help create a "situation comedy." An everyday place and a simple action can become a situation comedy. For example, you walk into a restaurant to buy a hamburger. You place your order but discover you lack six cents. You search the floor, find a nickel, and borrow a penny from the patron behind you. When you begin to eat, you discover that you forgot to request a hamburger without catsup and relish. When you are scraping off the unwanted condiments in the trash can, you accidentally drop the meat into the trash. After retrieving the hamburger, you discover that someone else is in your seat. You can continue to elaborate on the difficulties and add humor with unusual (abnormal) ways to resolve the problems. Silent film comedian Harold Lloyd (1894-1971) noted that "you get in a situation and you don't act as a normal person would."

☞ 2.   Identify the double lines of probability, idea of "the normal," and psychodynamic themes and in jokes, cartoons, or comic moments on television or film.

☞ 3.   Perform a commonplace activity (Exercise # 2 in Part I), and invent difficulties to doing the actions.

☞ 4.   Repeat Exercise #3, but with unusual or unexpected solutions to the problems you encounter.

ONE THING AT A TIME

Since the industrial revolution and the dawn of the machine age, an almost universal audience perspective developed about one thing — people are different from machines. The French critic Henri Bergson developed a theory of comedy based on the fact that the more a character's actions resemble those of a machine, the funnier the actions become. Bergson said what had become lost sight of in the age of the machine: people are laughable in situations where they behave in an automatic manner. When inflexible and rigid like machines, people lose their defining human characteristics of flexibility and versatility. In fact, Anthony M. Ludovici (1882–?) observed that, "we laugh when we feel that our adaptation to life is superior."[39] Comic characters are inferior in their ability to spontaneously adapt to the dynamic circumstances in which they find themselves.

Our human community upholds the norm of flexibility and versatility because the traits enable our species to survive. Thus, Cohan's number 15 can be funny if both the man and the woman move with machine-like precision with regard to both the distance and duration of their movements. Likewise, number 11 is funny if the man lights the cigar with machine-like regularity, each time convinced (erroneously) that he now understands how to successfully light the cigar.

The great French actor Jean-Louis Barrault (1910–) insists that "there should be deep in every actor, an element of the robot." Robots do actions sequentially rather than simultaneously; they do one thing at a time. Many great actors also do "one thing at a time," both to create a clear line of physical action to complement the line of psychological action created through their units of action, and to direct the audience's attention. With film and video, the camera operator and editor control the focus of the audience's attention. On stage, the actor alone must direct the audience's focus of attention. Simultaneous actions allow the audience to choose where to look; sequential actions give them no choice. The English stage director Tyrone Guthrie (1900–71) insisted:

> You learn how to do one important thing at a time. Beginners are forever trying to run to the door, open it and react to what they see, with gesture, facial expression and audible sounds, all at the same time. You must plan a sequence of impressions for the audience . . . [40]

Actors, especially comic actors, need to develop selectivity for sequential action. Distracting small actions can pull the audience's attention away from the particular elements needed to allow two perspectives to collide in the audience's brain. When effective, sequential action — doing one thing at a time — does not appear sequential; it just looks clean and beautiful. Watch the great silent film comedians, like Charles Chaplin (1889–1977) and Buster Keaton, to see how doing one thing at a time clarifies and magnifies their action.

☞ 5. Repeat Exercise # 4, with actions sequential rather than simultaneous. Do one thing at a time.

☞ 6. Repeat Exercise #5 with another actor performing her or his everyday activity. Perform the exercise with the attitude that the other actor is either more [-] or [+] than you are.

THE VAUDEVILLE TAKE

The "Vaudeville Take" clarifies both the double perspective of comedy and the comic character's relationship with the audience. The steps of the take are:

a. Character A reacts to Character B by looking down at the floor or at her feet.

b. Character A looks at Character B who has just spoken or acted.

c. Character A look at a "friend" in the audience.

d. Character A looks back to Character B on stage.

e. Character A looks back to the floor or at her feet.

f. Character A raises her head to speak her line either to Character B or to the audience.

In step A, Character A acknowledges that Character B is unaware of the "normal" perspective. With step B, Character A verifies Character B's ignorance. Step C seeks to establish a bond between Character A and the "normal" perspective of the audience. In step D, Character A seeks to cast Character B as an "ignorant" outsider. In step E, Character A considers the appropriate response to the situation. With step F, Character A returns to the action of the play. The Vaudeville Take often appears among the interactions of Stan Laurel, Oliver Hardy, and the movie audience, or among Ralph Kramden, Alice Kramden, and The Honeymooners' television audience. In some instances, the character doing the take is correct in placing himself in alliance with the audience; in other instances, the character is ignorant of the fact that the audience shares the perspective of the other character. Ralph may try to put down Alice, but he only reveals his own ignorance in the process.

☞   7.   Repeat Exercise #6. This time discover, but repeatedly deny to the other actor, through your actions, that the activity is more difficult than you believed it would be. It seems that everything that could go wrong, does go wrong. You may be unaware of the source of your difficulties. In addition, the problems you have drive you absolutely crazy—crazier than they would a "normal" person.

☞ 8. Repeat Exercise #2 from Part I but seek to accomplish the task in a way your audience would consider abnormal, illogical, unacceptable, or tasteless. Perform the actions, while believing that your way is the only normal, logical, acceptable, and tasteful way to proceed. You cannot understand what the audience finds funny about what you are doing. In fact, their laughter annoys, puzzles, or angers you.

☞ 9. Repeat Exercise #8 with another actor performing Exercise #8. Each of you should pursue an objective that either engages you with the other actor's activity or engages the other actor with your activity.

☞ 10. Repeat Exercise #6 from Part I. Incorporate the Vaudeville Take.

☞ 11. Repeat Exercise #10 using a pair of comic lines from Appendix 5. Add another pair of lines. Eventually you may say any line in any order, after repeating what you hear, and when something happens to make you.

ENERGY, EMOTION, AND SUBTEXT

The British actress Lynn Redgrave (1943–) believes that comedy is the most difficult form of drama to act; "it takes more energy and a stronger concentration."[41] Comedian Milton Berle (1908–) explains why: "You use more technique in trying to be funny and get laughs than in doing straight parts."[42] Incongruity invades every part of an actor's work. When the audience would expect a character to panic, the character relaxes. When the audience expects indifference, the character shows enthusiasm. Comic characters seem to react more violently to little things — a bottle cap elicits more fury than losing one's job. Little things seem to drive comic characters crazy. The "stakes are high" for seemingly insignificant things. As the critic John Lahr (1941–) wrote, "comedy is a game that's best when tense."[43]

When considering subtexts, comic actors seek ulterior levels of action incongruous with the textual level. For example, Bert Lahr's vow to "Punch ya silly!" as the Cowardly Lion in *The Wizard of Oz* is accompanied by a backward walk; his strong text is paired with a weak physical action for comic effect. In my high school, a particular student was notorious for waving his arm, only to declare "I don't know" when called upon to answer the teacher's question. His strong physical action and weak text always brought laughter. As Buster Keaton concluded, "the unexpected was our staple product, the unusual our object, and the unique was the ideal we were always hoping to achieve."[44]

☞   12.   Repeat Exercise #11 sequentially, with properties, verbal observations, and intentions, but with attention to an incongruous emotional preparation and incongruous subtexts.

COMIC TRAITS

In *The Poetics*, Aristotle suggests that a character can be like us, worse than us, or better than us. (This notion elaborates on psychodynamic traits #2, #3, #5, #6, and #7.) Consequently, actors developing comic characters have several choices when developing the principle of incongruity and the double perspective:

You, the character, **believe**:

1. You are like us, but **are** (from the audience's perspective) worse than us.

2. You are like us, but **are** (from the audience's perspective) better than us.

3. You are better than us, but **are** (from the audience's perspective) like us.

4. You are better than us, but **are** (from the audience's perspective) worse than us.

5. You are worse than us, but **are** (from the audience's perspective) like us.

6. You are worse than us, but **are** (from the audience's perspective) better than us.

As you consider examples of comic characters who fit each category, notice the different qualities of laughter each combination evokes. Also note that comic characters can be "better" or "worse" in many different ways. Aristotle defined comedy as "an imitation of [people] worse than average."[45]

Playwrights choose and assign traits to characters to make them "better" or "worse." Actors creating comic characters choose and assume traits, as well. An old adage about comic characters can help pinpoint the key traits to exploit: *find what is painful for the character*. In *Dumb and Dumber*, Lloyd Christmas' admission of the pain of a loveless life convinces his friend to go to Aspen with him. The rehearsal of comedy involves endless experimentation with different combinations of traits, seeking to turn a character's pain into an audience's pleasure. There are several basic kinds of traits:

Biological

Physical

Social

Dispositional

Deliberative

Biological traits give the character a being. Comic characters may misperceive the nature of their being. For example, you, the character either **believe**, or **must convince** others, that

You are a human, (but **are**, in reality, an animal).

You are a human, (but **are** in reality, an alien).

You are an animal, (but **are**, in reality, a human).

You are an alien, (but **are**, in reality, a human).

You are a woman, (but **are**, in reality, a man).

You are a man, (but **are**, in reality, a woman).

You are gay, (but **are**, in reality, heterosexual).

You are heterosexual, (but **are**, in reality, gay).

In movie jargon, these are "fish out of water" situations. Biological are the most fundamental traits and serve as the basis of both juvenile and classical comedy. Mickey Mouse is a rodent with human traits. Mork from Ork was television's alien mistaken for a human being by Mindy. In *Charley's Aunt*, *Tootsie*, and *The Birdcage*, a man must convince others that he is a woman. In Shakespeare's *Twelfth Night*, a woman must convince others that she is a man.

Often comic characters are compared to, or remind us, of animals or inanimate objects. These comparisons or associations provide actors with opportunities to absorb some of the physical characteristics of the object or animal into their own bodies and voices. Sometimes properties associated with a comic character can be used for the technique of **metaphor absorption**:

1. Study the actual animal or object closely, attending to your sensory reactions. What colors does it have? What do you associate with the colors? How does it feel? How does it smell? What do you associate with those sensations? How does it taste? What do you associate with that taste? Mirror the sensations with your face.

2. How does the animal or object move? How could it move? Move like the object could move. Run as if you were the object? Dance as if you were the object. Walk, run, dance, sit and rise as if you were a human being with these movement qualities.

3. What sounds does the animal or object make? What sounds could it make? Make sounds like the object does or could make. Sing, laugh, and cry as if you were the object. Talk, yell, whisper. laugh, cry, and sing as if you were a human being with these vocal qualities.

☞ 13. Repeat Exercise #12 with abstracted metaphorical speech and movement qualities taken from your analysis of biological traits.

Physical traits are any particular physical quality, such as age, size, weight, coloring, voice, physical ability, clothing, health, appearance, or accent. For example, an actor working on a comic character's misperceptions could explore many possibilities, among them:

You, the character **believe**, or **must convince** others, that

1. You are younger than you are, or than "normal."

2. You are older than you are, or than "normal."

3. You are larger than you are, or than "normal."

4. You are smaller than you are, or than "normal."

5. You are darker than you are, or than "normal."

6. You are lighter than you are, or than "normal."

7. You have a better voice than you do, or than "normal."

8. You have less of an accent than you do, or than "normal."

9. You are more agile than you are, or than "normal."

10. You are less agile than you are, or than "normal."

11. You are healthier than you are, or than "normal."

12. You are sicker than you are, or than "normal."

13. You are more beautiful than you are, or than "normal."

14. You are less beautiful than you are, or than "normal."

15. You are wealthier than you are, or than "normal."

16. You are poorer than you are, or than "normal."

Generally speaking, a comic character can believe that he or she is less or more "normal," physically, in a particular way, than he or she really is from the audience's perspective. Both "Three's Company"'s Mr. Furley and the Commedia dell'arte's Pantalone act younger than they are. Tom Hanks in *Big* and Peanuts' Lucy act older than they are. Alfalfa of *The Little Rascals* thought he had a more beautiful voice than he did. Steve Martin's (1945–) *The Jerk* believes he is more agile than he is. Both television's Fred Sanford and Molière's *Imaginary Invalid* believe themselves to be iller than they are. "The Golden Girls'" Blanche believes she is more beautiful than she is.

"Normal" (it cannot be overemphasized) is always relative to the particular audience whose perspective measures the characters' misperceptions. Dark, beautiful, and healthy for one audience may be light, ugly, and ill for another audience. **Know your audience or the comic effect will not occur.** The American director Stuart Vaughn (1925–) recalls advice given by the American author/actor Howard Lindsay (1889–1968):

> "If you can't amuse them, convince them." He meant that if, when you start the evening, they just aren't laughing as fully as usual, don't try to be funnier—don't push.

> Just play as truthfully as you can, and you will gradually
> draw them in . . . . [46]

☞ 14. Repeat Exercise # 12 with a misperception of a biological trait.

☞ 15. Repeat Exercise # 14 with a partner without a misperception of a biological trait (a "normal" person).

☞ 16. Repeat Exercise #12 with a misperception of a physical trait.

☞ 17. Repeat Exercise # 16 with a partner who does not
misperceive a physical trait (a "normal" person).

☞ 18. Dialects are considered "abnormal." Repeat Exercise
12 with a dialect.[47]

☞ 19. Repeat exercise #18 with a partner who does not
have a dialect.

Social traits give characters social positions and relationships.
"Daughter," "father," "debtor," "creditor," "sage," "fool," "doctor,"
"lawyer," and "Indian chief" are a few examples of characters defined
by a social trait. Characters are often comic when placed in incongruous social positions and relationships: the farmer, Strepsiades, as a lo-
gician in *The Clouds*; Bottom the Ass as the Fairy Queen's lover and
Bottom the Weaver as tragic thespian in *A Midsummer Night's Dream*;
Jack Horner as *The Country Wife*'s eunuch; Azdak the Judge of *The
Caucasian Chalk Circle*; Groucho as chief of state; the Three Stooges as
high society diners; Lucy as assembly line worker; Roseanne as de-
partment store Santa; street hustler Sinbad as a world famous dentist
in *Houseguest*; and Whoopie Goldberg as nun. The film comedy *Dumb
and Dumber* is based on this trait.

Some psychologists have analyzed drama by social role. For example, Sigmund Freud (1856–1939) described as tragic those characters
who feel guilt over a desire to play their parents' social role. Hamlet,
for example, desiring to replace his father, and Electra, desiring to re-

place her mother, rebel against the social norm. Likewise, Ludwig Jekels (1867–1954) described as comic those characters who desire to play their children's social roles. For example, in *The School for Wives*, Molière's old Arnolphe seeks to replace the young Horace as the lover of his ward Agnes. Horace, the potent child, acts mature, while Arnolphe, the impotent father, acts immature. In tragedy, the child figure, sensing an increase in power, rebels against the social "norm"; in comedy, the parent figure, sensing a loss of power, rebels against the social "norm." Like Agnes, Roseanne's and Homer Simpson's television children are often mortified by their parents' "immature" behavior.

In *Beyond Laughter*, psychologist Martin Grotjahn (1904–90) points out that historically the clown has represented a "depreciated" parent figure. The medieval fool's costume, for example — tassels drooping from the cap, and the fool's scepter (a laughable penis) — was full of symbols of castration and impotence. The symbols of phallic impotence continue with Groucho Marx's (1891–1977) cigar, W. C. Fields' (1870–1946) pool cue, Charlie Chaplin's cane, and Oliver Hardy's (1892–1957) necktie. The male clown's pants and the female clown's hose are baggy because the old owners can no longer fill their social role costumes. The red phallic nose on the male clown and the giant vaginal red-lip-sticked mouth on the female clown testify to the comic characters' determination to preserve their fading potency at all costs. The female clown sports a wilted flower on her cap, giant hanging breasts, a balloon rump. Today comic Judy Tenuta (1951–), the "love goddess," is never seen without her "squeeze box" accordion. If sex seems to be everywhere remember Robert Orben's (1927–) observation: "Life itself is off-color and sex and sexual behavior will always interest people."[48]

Children who act like adults may also be comic characters. The Peanuts characters, Bart Simpson, and Lily Tomlin's (1939–) Edith Ann are examples of children whose adult-like dispositions and deliberative traits create laughter because of the incongruity. Early film comedies, like *The Little Rascals*, based their humor on the same incongruity. The characters avoid tragedy by their lack of a desire to re-place their actual parents.

Martin Grotjahn acknowledges the sadness and pain underlying the comic characters' inability to change, to adapt to the aging processes of life. To him, the clown "also represents the sadness of things and finally comes to stand for death in the person of the tragic truly great clown. This is the point where tragedy and comedy finally meet and symbolize human life."[49]

Dispositional traits reflect a character's basic mood or bent. The comedian Flip Wilson (1933–) observed "Funny is an attitude." But comic characters do not know they are in a comedy. Indeed, the great English actor Charles Laughton (1899–1962) observed, "You play a tragedy like a comedy and you play a comedy like a tragedy." The American clown Emmett Kelly (1898–1979) also cautioned would-be comedians: "one of the fundamentals of clowning is to start out doing something that looks serious and then have it pay off in a ridiculous manner."[50] Often comic characters believe they have dispositions different from the ones seen by the audience. For example,

You, the character believe that you are.

Happy, but the audience sees you as sad.

Sad, but the audience sees you as happy.

Reasonable, but the audience sees you as irrational.

Intellectual, but the audience sees you as ignorant.

Mannered, but the audience sees you as boorish.

Humorous, but the audience sees you as embarrassing.

Winsome, but the audience sees you as morose.

Generous, but the audience sees you as stingy.

Sometimes characters' names give clues to their disposition: Lady Wishfort, Mr. Pinchwife, Mr. Horner, Sir Belch, Sir Aguecheek, Mistress Chat, Mrs. Sullen. Other times, characters' names are ironic. In addition, comic characters rarely seem to make transitions between moods; their changes are abrupt, sudden, and seemingly unmotivated.

Deliberative traits refer to the kind of thinking in which a character engages. There are two basic ways of thinking — expediently and ethically. Expedient thinking considers how to do something. Ethical thought considers whether or not something should be done. Comic characters often engage in one kind of deliberation when the other kind would be more appropriate. In addition, comic characters tend to spend more time on expedient deliberations and less time on ethical thinking — the opposite of what one may expect from "normal" people.

COMIC INVENTION

When the famed character actor Edmund Gwenn (1875–1959) was dying, his friends gathered at his bedside for a deathwatch. One of them asked, "Tell me, Edmund, is dying hard?' Gwenn thought a moment and then said, "Yes . . . but not as hard as comedy."

When working on comic characters, actors need to spent countless hours experimenting with various combination of traits and techniques. As Buster Keaton advised, "try anything at all."[51] The great American comedy writer Robert Orben noted that "your highest compliment as a comedian is to be called a jerk."[52] The American comedian Danny Thomas (1914–91) observed that a comic character's identity can arise through the repeated doing and saying of small things — "it's what you say and how you say it that gets you to where you become a who . . . and when you become a who your material doesn't have to be as good."[53]

Comic actors work on how they do things. The great American comedian Ed Wynn's (1886-1966) epigram is defining: **A comic says funny things and a comedian says things funny.** Comedian Milton Berle (1908–) elaborates: "a comic is a guy who depends solely on the joke, and we have thousands of them. The comedian can get a laugh opening a door in the funny way that he does it and his attitude — that's a comic versus a comedian. Now a funnyman can get a laugh before he opens his mouth."[54] To this end, the great American comedian Ed Wynn — "the perfect fool" — had a large collection of funny hats; a comic just saves jokes. Seinfeld's Cosmo Kramer gets laughs before he says a word.

☞ 20. Experiment with various combinations of comic devices (difficulty with activity, a-normal problem-solving, vaudeville takes, incongruous emotional state and subtexts, a-normal biological trait, a-normal physical trait, dialect) to create a comic character. Place your character in a familiar scene with a "normal" character, i.e., on a game show like "Wheel of Fortune" or "Jeopardy"; at a job interview, marriage counseling session, or dating service. Always seek to make your actions sequential.

☞ 21. Enter as the comic character you have been developing. Justify stopping, looking at the audience, and exiting. Your goal should be to elicit laughter through your manner of doing things.

☞ 22. Repeat Exercise #21 with a funny hat.

☞ 23. Repeat Exercise #22 with a partner. Enter, look at each other, look at the audience, exchange a comic loop (see Appendix 5) and exit sequentially.

☞ 24. Experiment with various combinations of the comic devices (difficulty with activity, a-normal problem-solving, vaudeville takes, incongruous emotional state and subtexts, a-normal biological trait, a-normal physical trait, dialect) to create a comic character. Use the line comic pairs of Appendix 5 as the basis of the scene's vocabulary.

COMIC DICTION

Like all language for the stage, the diction of comedy is heightened diction, words and phrases different from those we use in everyday life. Even language which seems everyday, has been shaped and selected to convey the precise information in the appropriate rhythm. (An introduction to the basis features of heightened diction is available in Part I.) In addition to the verbal conceits available to all drama, comedy employs additional figures of speech:

Adianoeta — an expression with two meanings. To an unsuccessful applicant, a foundation writes, "For your work, we have nothing but praise."

Anachronism — something placed in an inappropriate period of time.

Antithesis — Jackie "Moms" Mabley (1897–1975): "A woman is a woman until the day she dies, but a man's a man only as long as he can" and "There ain't nothin' an ol' man can do but bring me a message from a young one."

Antonomasia — The use of a descriptive phrase as a proper name. (See section on character names.)

Asteismus — A mocking, smart-assed reply, focusing on one word. "Did you pass the salt?" "How fast was it going?"

Auxesis — Hyperbole; exaggeration for effect; an overstatement. In *Mules and Men* (1935), Zora Neale Hurston (1903–60) writes, "My old man had some land dat was so rich dat our mule died and we buried him down in our bottom land, and de next mornin' he had done sprouted l'il jackasses." There's also Muhammad Ali's (1942–) "I'm so fast I could hit you before God gets the news."

Barbarismus — mispronunciation through ignorance. In singing "Let's Call the Whole Thing Off," the auditioner pronounces "tomato" the same way each time it is sung.

Bathos — a sudden and ridiculous descent from the exalted to the ordinary; when striving for the noble, the ludicrous is achieved. Aristophanes' (c. 448–c. 380 B.C.E.) *The Congresswomen* opens with Praxagora's invocation to her nightlamp:

> "O beam resplendent, blaze of glazed gaze, O horribly gorgeous orb, who wheeled and sprang, the fairest ware of those who live for the kiln, O Bedside Lamp. . .(I really feel I should divulge your parentage and fate; you've come so far from low beginnings.)"

Bomphiologia — Bombastic speech, inappropriate for either the speaker or the situation. The boastful coward Ralph Roister Doister vows "Yes, for although he had as many lives

> As a thousand widows, and a thousand wives,
> As a thousand lions, and a thousand rats,
> A thousand wolves, and a thousand cats,
> A thousand bulls, and a thousand calves,
> And a thousand legions divided in halves,
> He shall never scape death on my sword's point, —
> Though I should be torn therefore joint by joint!"

Doggerel — Rough, crudely written verse, usually intentionally or unintentionally humorous. Bottom the Weaver's opening soliloquy as Pyramus the Lover in Shakespeare's *A Midsummer Night's Dream* begins,

> O grim-looked night, O night with hue so black,
> O night which ever art when day is not;
> O night, O night, alack, alack, alack,
> I fear my Thisbe's promise is forgot.
> And thou, O wall, O sweet O lovely wall,
> That stand'st between her father's ground and mine,
> Thou wall, O wall, O sweet and lovely wall,
> Show me thy chink, to blink through with mine eyne."

Dozens (or Snaps) — "To play the dozens" is to play an elaborate word game of reciprocal insult, especially against an opponent's mother. The game is a test of emotional strength, since the loser is the one who angers first.

"Your mother is like a doorknob. Everybody gets a turn.
Your mother is like a piece of pie. Everybody gets a piece.
Your mother is like a dresser. Everyone gets into her drawers.
Your mother thinks she's sharp 'cause her head comes to a point.
Your mother thinks she's a big wheel because her face looks like a hubcap."[55]

Epigram — a short witty statement, graceful in style and ingenious in thought. An example is the English playwright Oscar Wilde's (1854–1900) "A man cannot be too careful in the choice of his enemies."

Euphemism — a roundabout expression to make the thought delicate and inoffensive. Examples would be "passed away" for "died" and "break wind" for "fart."

Hypophora — asking and immediately answering questions. In Act III of George Bernard Shaw's (1856–1950) *Man and Superman*, the Devil rants:

"This marvellous force of Life of which you boast is a force of Death: Man measures his strength by his destructiveness. What is his religion? An excuse for hating me. What is his law? An excuse for hanging you. What is his morality? Gentility! an excuse for consuming without producing. What is his art? An excuse for gloating over pictures of slaughter."

Invective — A linguistic attack seeking to ridicule. In her 1933 review of the play *The Lake*, Dorothy Parker (1893–1967) said, "Go to the Martin Beck Theatre and watch Katherine Hepburn run the gamut-t-t of emotion from A to B." In Harold Pinter's (1930–) *The Birthday Party*, Goldberg and McCann berate Stanley:

Goldberg: Where is your lechery leading you?
McCann: You'll pay for this.
Goldberg: You stuff yourself with dry toast.
McCann: You contaminate womankind.
Goldberg: Why don't you pay the rent?
McCann: Mother defiler!

> Goldberg: Why do you pick your nose?
>
> McCann: I demand justice!

In Shakespeare's *Henry IV*, Act II, Scene 5, Prince Harry and Sir John Falstaff banter:

> Prince Harry: How now, woolsack, what mutter you?
>
> Sir John: A king's son! If I do not beat thee out of thy kingdom with a dagger of lath, and drive all thy subjects afore thee like a flock of wild geese, I'll never wear hair on my face more. You, Prince of Wales!
>
> Prince Harry: Why, you whoreson round man, what's the matter?
>
> Sir John: Are you not a coward? Answer me to that.

Irony — saying the opposite of what is believed or felt. "Does it hurt? Only when I laugh." A subspecies of irony, **antiphrasis**, uses just one word, as in calling a dwarf a "giant."

Limerick — A form of light verse consisting of five anapestic lines (two unstressed syllables followed by one stressed syllable), rhyming A/A/B/B/A (the first, second and fifth lines rhyme and the third and fourth lines rhyme). The first, second and fifth lines are trimeter (have three metrical feet) and the third and fourth lines are dimeter (have two metrical feet). In George S. Kaufman (1889–1961) and Moss Hart's (1904–61) *You Can't Take It With You* the drunken actress Gay Wellington recites:

> There was a young lady from Wheeling
> Who had a remarkable feeling,
>   She laid on her back
>   And opened her crack
> And pissed all over the ceiling.

Litotes — To express a thought by denying its opposite. "He is not the wisest man in the world."

Malapropism — a linguistic blunder caused by substituting one word for another similar in sound but different in meaning. In Act III scene 3 of Richard Brinsley Sheridan's (1751–1816) *The Rivals*:

> Mrs. Malaprop: You are very good, and very consider-
> ate, Captain. I am sure I have done everything in
> my power since I **exploded** the affair! Long ago I
> laid my **positive conjunctions** on her never to
> think on the fellow again; I have since laid Sir An-
> thony's **preposition** before her; but, I'm sorry to
> say, she seems resolved to decline every **particle**
> that I enjoin her.

Movie mogul Samuel Goldwyn (1882–1974) said, "Include me out." Clever character's can deliberately coin malaprops. For example, playwright and actress Mae West (1893–1980) said, "She's the kind of woman who climbed the ladder of success, wrong by wrong." Comedy writer Jane Ace (1905–74) claimed, "I am a ragged individualist."

Nonce Word—a word invented for a particular occasion. In Walt Disney's *Mary Poppins* a song introduces "supercalifragilisticexpialidocious."

Nonsense Verse—verse in which sense and meaning is less important than sound. Lewis Carroll's (1832–98) *Jabberwocky* begins "'Twas brillig, and the slithy toves did gyre and gimble in the wabe."

Paradox—a statement which seems self-contradictory, but which reconciles the seeming opposites. British philosopher Bertrand Russell's (1872–1970) "There is no God, but Mary is his Mother" and the Slavic proverb, "Under capitalism man exploits man; under communism the reverse is true" are two examples.

Periphrasis—circumlocution; using more words than necessary to express an idea. The American humorist Ambrose Bierce (1842–1914) defined circumlocution as "a literary trick whereby the writer who has nothing to say breaks it gently to the reader." An example would be Doctor Johnson's (1709–84) reference to a sunset as "the gentle coruscations of declining day."

Portmanteau Word—a word formed by combining two or more words. "Guess" + "estimate" = "Guesstimate"; "Breakfast" + "Lunch" = "Brunch"

Pun—word play of four basic types:

1) **antanaclasis:** one word used in two different meanings. In Shakespeare's *Much Ado About Nothing* V, ii a pun is coined:

   Margaret: Well, I will call Beatrice to you, who I think hath legs.
   Benedick: And therefore will come."

2) **paronomasia:** two words pronounced the same, but with different meanings. In Shakespeare's *The Taming of the Shrew* V, ii another pun is introduced:

   Widow: Thus I conceive by him.
   Petruccio: Conceives by me! How likes Hortensio that?
   Hortensio: My widow says thus she conceives her tale."

3) **syllepsis** — a word brings together two constructions, each of which has a different meaning in connection with the yoking word. An example is Mae West's, "It's not the men in my life that counts, it's the life in my men."

4) **zeugma** — using a word in relationship with two others, but having the word only relate correctly to one of the words. "What housewives cannot eat, they can" or "He said as he hastily put out the cat, the wine, his cigar, and the lamps."

Repartee — a conversation of swift, witty replies. Writers Claire Boothe Luce (1903–87) and Dorothy Parker met in a nightclub doorway. "Age before beauty," said Luce as she offered Parker first entrance. "Pearls before swine," replied Parker as she accepted the offer.

Repetition — Benedict in *Much Ado About Nothing* II, iii: "One woman is fair, **yet I am well.** Another is wise, **yet I am well. Another** virtuous, **yet I am well.** But till all graces be in one woman, **one woman** shall not come in my **grace.**" Comedian Joey Adams: "Never let a fool kiss you or a kiss fool you."

Reversal — saying the opposite of what is expected. Dorothy Parker: "One more drink and I'll be under the host." Nipsey Russell (1925–): "He who turns the other cheek, gets hit with the other fist." Mae West: "He who hesitates — is a damn fool"; "Too much of a good thing can be wonderful." The English actress Mrs. Patrick Campbell (1865–1940) in a letter to playwright George Bernard Shaw: "Laugh and the world laughs with you, snore and you snore alone." As the comedian Buddy Young Jr. says in the film *Mr. Saturday Night*, "You see what I did there? You thought I was goin' . . . but I took you the other way."

Riddle — a puzzle in the form of a question. "Where was Moses when the lights went out? In the dark."

Sarcasm — bitter or derisive taunt. Theatre patron: "I'd like tickets as close to the front as possible because my friend is deaf." Box Office: "We don't have tickets that close."

Spoonerism — reversal of initial letters. In Aristophanes' *The Congresswomen*, Praxagora explains her plan: "We must dispone our limbs in crafty slyness on what the noted spoonerizer Phyromachos once deigned to name *those beery wenches*." Jane Ace combined spoonerism, pun and reversal with her "Time wounds all heels."

The most common type of comic language is the joke. Like comic characters, jokes depends upon the parallel existence of two perspectives or lines of probability. Jokes also have a structure. A clear analysis of the structure of a joke was offered to director Stuart Vaughn by actor Walter Young.[56] Young believed that most jokes have five parts: **The Plant, The Pause, The Point, The Amplifier, The Bridge**.

The Plant is the set up or given circumstances which establishes the first perspective or line of probability. To set up the joke, actors must not move during key words in The Plant. Here's a sample joke: An actor came to his apartment and found his spouse in bed with another actor. The actor said, "My God! What are you doing?" The other actor said— (So far the joke has touched upon psychodynamic traits #1, #2, #4, #6, #7, #8, and #10.) During The Plant, heed Robert Orben's advise: "Don't telegraph a joke. In other words, don't tell the joke in such a way the audience will know what the punchline is going to be. If they start to laugh during your set-up line, something's wrong."[57]

The Pause is a hesitation which invites the audience to complete or fill in the rest of the perspective or conclude the line of probability.

Comic actors usually freeze during The Pause, holding just long enough for suspense, but not long enough for the audience to guess the hidden perspective.

The Point reveals the alternate perspective or line of probability. As with The Plant, key words need to be emphasized by physical stillness. The Point is sometimes called the Punchline or Tag: "Well, next week I'm doing a soap. Then I have a picture. Then I . . . ." (This particular Point adds psychodynamic theme #3 to the picture.) Psychologist Gerald W. Grumet explains the physiological effect of the point: "As the 'punchline' is sprung, the comedian stuns his audience with a libidinal absurdity; a sudden shift occurs from a neutral idea to a cathected idea . . . . The cerebral cortex, normally able to maintain inhibitory control over libidinized subcortical centers, momentarily loses its dominance, allowing discharge of the lower centers which occurs in the form of laughter, until inhibitory control is reestablished."[58]

The Amplifier is a physical reaction or auditory punctuation to The Point. The stillness during The Point focuses the audience on The Amplifier. The Vaudeville Take or a drum "rimshot" are common amplifiers. A joke onstage needs a character, other than the speaker, to react to The Point for the audience to fully experience the humorous incongruity. Dr. Grumet explains that "the laugh response is often further prompted by an intense sensory stimulus, such as a drum roll, creating a startle response to further heighten arousal."

The Bridge is transitional dialogue or business which moves the action from one joke to another. "But what did your wife do?" "My wife? You should have my wife. Listen, my wife is so . . . " Do not begin The Bridge too soon. Robert Orben cautions: "Never step on a laugh. There is a psychological moment for beginning your next gag. This occurs at a point just following the peak of your audience's laughter. The laughs haven't stopped as yet, but they're diminishing in volume. When this moment is reached, go into your next line. If you start too soon, you'll cut off the audience's full enjoyment of the line. If you wait too long, there'll be a moment of awkward silence that'll give your audience a chance to cool off."[59]

COMEDY AND CLARITY

Since comedy depends upon directing the audience's attention toward one perspective, in order to surprise it with another perspective, actors need to be sure that the audience focus does not wander. To control the audience's attention, actors need to control their own actions and to coordinate their actions with those of their partner. Small foot or hand movements, called the "dirt" of acting by Constantin Stanislavski (1863–1938), can blur the audience's focus and kill the humor. Comic actors need to do less, as little as possible, in fact. Actions need precision, control, shape, and clarity.

Even with the words, comic actors need clarity and precision. Robert Orben warns: "Don't ever stumble over a line because you've forgotten it. Comedy has to be spontaneous. Any hesitation in the delivery of a gag kills the laugh. You must know your lines so well, nothing can make you forget them."[60] Playwright Larry Gelbart (1923–), observed that "you don't buy a finely jeweled watch and put two more parts into it"; the language of comedy is as precise as the watch and needs the same care.

COMIC CHARACTER ANALYSIS

Robert Orben advises would-be comedians that "your first step is to make thoroughly sure that you understand the material."[61] Since comedy needs a double perspective, actors need to create two analyses when working on a comic character. One analysis sees the situation from the character's perspective and follows the form of Appendix 3. The second analysis establishes the incongruities and is written from the actor/audience perspective. Unlike the first analysis, the second analysis uses the third person singular pronouns "he" or "she," thereby giving the actor a more objective view of the work.

CHARACTER	ACTOR/AUDIENCE
Who am I?	Who is he/she really?
What do I want?	What does she/he really want?
Why do I want what I want?	Why does he/she really want it?
What obstacles stand in my way?	What obstacles are unknown to her/him?
What am I willing to do to get what I want?	What is he/she really willing to do?
How do I plan to attain each of my goals?	
	How does she/he really plan to attain her/his goals? How should she/he have pursued her/his goals?
What are the verbal conceits?	
What important discoveries do I make?	What are the verbal mistakes?
	What mistaken discoveries were made? What discoveries should he/she have made?
What important decisions do I make?	What were the wrong decisions she/he made? What important decisions should she/he have made?
What is the basis of each decision?	How does he/she misperceive his/her situation with regard to time and place?
How do the specific time and place affect my actions?	What traits does she/he misperceive about herself/himself? What incongruous social traits does she/he assume?

☞ 25. Analyze a character from a comedy according to Exercise # 36 in Part 1.

☞ 26. Part I Exercise # 37 for the comic character.

☞ 27. Part I Exercise # 38 for the comic character.

☞ 28. In a journal, record examples of comic incongruity which you see, hear, or read. Apply the principles practiced in analyzing the comedy you encounter.

EXERCISES

A BASIC WARM UP

1. Stand in a centered, aligned position. Let your shoulders drop. Roll them, circle them. Swing your arms around.

2. Drop your head to your chest. Roll it round on your neck.

3. Tense up all your face muscles, then relax them. Repeat this a few times. Massage your face.

4. Stretch you face muscles. Rotate your jaw making sighing sounds all the while.

5. Stretch your whole body in every direction, uttering big voiced yawns all the while. Repeat several times.

6. Swing various parts of your body in the rhythm of your breathing.

7. Stick your tongue out as far as possible. Try to get the whole tongue out.

8. Bounce in place, then shake every part of your body.

9. Shake your hands at their wrists as hard as you can for a while. Then reach and stretch one arm after the other toward the ceiling. Repeat a few times.

10. Shout out lines of text as loudly as possible, then as rapidly as possible, then as slowly as possible. Explore the bounds and varieties of movement as you do.

11. Articulate assorted tongue twisters while enacting their contents as physically as possible. (*Five pleasant pheasant pluckers; The sixth sheik's sixth sheep's sick; Does your shirt shop stock socks with spots? I bought a box of biscuits, a box of mixed biscuits, and a biscuit mixer; I slit the sheet and the sheet slit me — slitten was the sheet that was slit by me.*)

OPEN SCENE 1

A: So?

B: Ready?

A: No.

B: I see.

A: Yes.

B: Why are you doing this?

A: It's the best thing.

B: You can't mean it.

A: I'm serious.

B: You shouldn't...

A: What? Go on.

B: It's nothing.

A: What?

B: Forget it.

A: Okay.

OPEN SCENE 2

A: So?

B: Ready?

C: Well.

A: No.

C: Oh, yes.

B: I see.

A: Yes.

B: Why are you doing this?

C: You can't mean it.

A: It's the best thing.

C: See.

B: You can't mean it.

A: I'm serious.

B: You shouldn't . . .

A: What? Go on.

C: Take it easy.

B: It's nothing.

A: What?

B: Forget it.

A: Okay.

C: That's easy for you to say.

OPEN SCENE A E

A: So please you?

B: Are you so?

A: Nay.

B: I see.

A: Ay.

B: Wherefore dost thou this?

A: 'Tis best.

B: Thou canst not mean so.

A: Truly.

B: Forbear thy...

A: What would you? Speak again.

B: 'Tis naught.

A: What wilt thou?

B: Think not on't.

A: So be it.

OPEN SCENE B E

A: So please you?

B: Are you so?

C: Ay, marry.

A: Nay.

C: Ay, 'tis thus.

B: I see.

A: Ay.

B: Wherefore dost thou this?

C: Thou canst not mean so.

A: 'Tis best.

C: Look on't.

B: Thou are not so resolved.

A: Truly.

B: Forbear thy...

A: What would you? Speak again.

C: Soft, sirrah.

B: 'Tis naught.

A: What wilt thou?

B: Think not on't.

A: So be it.

C: Thou dost speak fairly.

CHARACTER ANALYSIS CHECKLIST

Who am I?

    Name.

    Family.

    Age.

    Significant physical traits.

    Significant relationships.

        What do I need from each?

        What do I get from each?

        Changes in the play.

        Changes in the scene.

    Disposition: Polar Attitudes

        What do you think of yourself?

        What do you think of others?

        Change in the play.

        Change in the scene.

What do I want?

    From the play as a whole: superobjective

    In this scene: intentions

    Why do I want what I want?

What obstacles stand in my way?

    In the play.

    In this scene.

What am I willing to do to get what I want?

How do I plan to attain each of my goals?

What are the verbal conceits I choose?

What important discoveries do I make?

What important decisions do I make? What is the basis of each decision?

How do the specific time and place affect my actions?

✧ ✧ ✧ ✧ ✧

Where have I been prior to each entrance?

What was I doing there?

Why did I decide to come here now?

How do I feel?

What do I plan to do here?

Whom do I expect to find here?

What do need or want from each?

How will I know that I have succeeded?

What makes me stay here after I enter?

✧ ✧ ✧ ✧ ✧

To engage your non-verbal creativity, undertake the following activities:

Make a collage of your character.

Draw a relationship map of your character.

PART THREE

If your character were a game piece, make a gameboard for the play.

Describe the setting with as much sensory detail as you can.

Generate metaphors about your character:

"He walks like a _____,"

"She talks like a _____,"

"If he were an animal he'd be a _____,"

"If she were a color she'd be _____"

Use a metaphor to describe each of your character's relationships: "The relationship between me and _____ is like the relationship between _____ and _____." Explain each.

Color your script. Use a different color for intentions, obstacles, discoveries, decisions, and each kind of verbal conceit.

JABBERWOCKY

'Twas brillig, and the slithy toves
Did gyre and gimble in the wabe:
All mimsy were the borogroves,
And the mome wraths outgrabe.

"Beware the Jabberwock, my son!
The jaws that bite, the claws that catch!
Beware the Jubjub bird, and shun
The frumious Bandersnatch!"

He took his vorpal sword in hand:
Long time the manxome foe he sought-
So rested he by the Tumtum tree,
And stood awhile in thought.

And, as in uffish thought he stood,
The Jabberwock, with eyes of flame,
Came whiffling through the tulgey wood,
And burbled as it came!

One, two! One, two! And through and through
The vorpal blade went snicker-snack!
He left it dead, and with its head
He went galumphing back.

"And hast thou slain the Jabberwock?
Come to my arms, my beamish boy!
O frabjous day! Calooh! Callay!
He chortled in his joy.

'Twas brillig, and the slithy toves
Did gyre and gimble in the wabe:
All mimsy were the borogroves,
And the mome wraths outgrabe.

Lewis Carroll

DICTION LOOPS

The following pairs of lines should be played as a looped conversation. Repeat what you hear from your perspective and remember to wait for something to happen before you go on with your line.

A: What does it look like to you?

B: I'm not sure.

******

A: I'm still scared.

B: I'm not scared.

******

A: Stop it.

B: I can't.

******

A: Harder.

B: I am.

******

A: It broke.

B: I'll fix it.

******

A: What do you mean?

B: Never mind.

A: What time is it?

B: Eleven.

******

A: See for yourself.

B: I believe you.

******

A: This is it.

B: You're sure.

******

A: Goodbye.

B: Wait.

******

A: Listen.

B: I don't hear anything.

******

A: Sure I have.

B: When?

******

A: Where's it coming from?

B: I don't know.

******

A: Don't worry.

B: That's easy for you to say.

A: I can't do it.

B: You can.

******

A: I don't think so.

B: Why not?

******

A: Don't worry.

B: I'm not worried.

******

A: Maybe you should.

B: I don't think so.

******

A: Forget it.

B: I don't mind.

******

A: What observation mad'st thou in this case?

B: The day that she was missing he was here.

******

A: Then swore he that he was a stranger here.

B: Call it by what you will, the day is yours.

******

A: With what persuasion did he tempt thy love?

B: Sit with my cousin. Lend him your kind pains.

A: This favor will I do you for his sake.

B: To say you're welcome were superfluous.

ooo

A: Look that you take upon as you should.

B: Then go with me to make the matter good.

ooo

A: I prithee go and get me some repast.

B: I'll leave you. Pray you speak to'em, I pray you.

ooo

A: They did not bless us with one happy word.

B: It is thy business that I go about.

ooo

A: I am a fool, and full of poverty.

B: Search every acre in the high-grown field.

ooo

A: Let us confess and turn it to a jest.

B: When I am known aright, you shall not grieve.

ooo

A: Here I stand, lady, dart thy skill at me.

B: By heaven, I love thee better than myself.

ooo

A: Bruise me with scorn, confound me with flour.

B: Obey and go with me, for thou must die.

A: Thrust thy sharp wit quite through my ignorance.

B: Can vengeance be pursued further than death?

ooo

A: Cut me to pieces with thy keen conceit.

B: Your looks I fear, and your intents I doubt.

ooo

A: O, never will I trust to speeches penned.

B: I will be gone, sir, and not trouble ye.

ooo

A: My love to thee is sound, sans crack or flaw.

B: By heaven, I will tear thee joint by joint.

ooo

A: Thy words are but as thoughts, therefore be bold.

B: They are infected; in their heart it lies.

ooo

A: I thank you, sir, and pray you tell me this.

B: But what a' God's name doth become of this?

ooo

A: I shall desire more love and knowledge of you.

B: It must be so. Content thyself.

ooo

A: Let me the knowledge of my fault bear with me.

B: Well hast thou spoken, cousin. Be it so.

A: Let it suffice thee that I trust thee not.

B: If I be not, heavens be revenged upon me.

ooo

A: What's that to me? My father was no traitor.

B: Thy father was a traitor to the crown.

ooo

A: What see'st thou there. King Henry's diadem.

B: I was to young that time to value you.

ooo

A: A day will come when you will claim your own.

B: Achilles shall have word of this intent.

ooo

A: I'll to the Duke of Suffolk presently.

B: Yourself shall feast with us before you go.

ooo

A: I cannot blame you all. What's it to you?

B: But you already are too insolent.

ooo

A: There's nothing here that is too good for you.

B: There's reason you should be displeased at it.

ooo

A: My being here it is that holds thee hence..

B: I pray you stay not, but in haste to horse.

A: Do with your injuries as seems you best.

B: O that it were as like as it is true!

******

A: This is strange abuse. Let's see thy face.

B: Go thou toward home, where I will never come.

******

A: Do you smoke after sex?

B: No, but I sizzle a little.

******

A: How do I get to Carnegie Hall?

B: Practice.

******

A: Does your watch tell time?

B: No, I have to look at it.

A: I'll dance on your grave.

B: Then I'll be buried at sea.

******

A: I haven't eaten in four days.

B: Force yourself.

******

A: Will you pass the salt?

B: How fast is it going?

A: I almost got killed twice today.

B: Once would have been enough.

******

A: Do you like bathing beauties?

B: I don't know. I've never bathed any.

******

A: Do you have a peacock?

B: What do you think-I squirt it out of my navel?

******

A: Will you give me a buck for a sandwich?

B: Let me see the sandwich.

******

A: Your shoes are on the wrong feet.

B: These are the only feet I have.

A: Will you love me forever?

B: I'd like to, but I have a nine-o-clock class.

******

A: It hurts when I do that.

B: Then don't do that.

******

A: Do you love driving.

B: Well, I usually stop first.

A: How much did Phil leave when he died?

B: Everything.

******

A: There's a ringing in my ears.

B: Don't answer it.

******

A: Are papayas healthy?

B: I've never heard one complain.

******

A: Why don't you take a bus home?

B: You would never let me keep it.

******

A: I'm my own worst enemy.

B: Not when I'm around.

******

A: Am I hard to please?

B: I don't know. I've never tried.

******

A: Am I too late for the garbage?

B: No, jump in.

******

A: My mother made me a homosexual.

B: Would she make one for me, too?

A: I just set my hair.

B: What time does it go off?

******

A: Do you suffer from insanity?

B: No, I enjoy every minute of it.

******

A: What was your last position?

B: Missionary.

******

A: What's this fly doing in my soup?

B: The backstroke.

******

A: Where were you between five and six?

B: Kindergarten.

A: Will you join me in a bowl of soup?

B: There isn't enough room for one of us.

******

A: Have an accident?

B: No thanks. Just had one.

******

A: Nobody takes me seriously.

B: No kidding?

A: I should have listened to my father ten years ago.

B: Go ahead. He's still talking.

******

A: If you don't stop, I'll kill myself.

B: Promises, promises.

******

A: I have ten children to feed. What'll I do?

B: Haven't you done enough?

******

A: You have too many roaches in here.

B: How many am I allowed?

******

A: When's your brother getting married?

B: All the time.

COMEDY WARM-UPS

Psychologists have identified the acts most amusing to infants.[62] Play them with a partner to get in the appropriate child-like creative frame of mind. Repeat each exercise until you have succeeded in making your partner laugh. Combine exercises for variety and surprise. When warming up for a performance, play the exercises as your comic character.

1. *Gonna Get Ya*. Wiggle your finger in the air, while saying "I'm" musically, and then poke or tickle your partner gently in the stomach as you say "gonna get ya."

2. *Kissing Tummy*. Four quick kisses on your partner's bare stomach.

3. *Walking Fingers*. Walk two fingers slowly toward your partner to give a gentle poke in the ribs. Repeat the walk, slower or faster, adding silly sounds, and talking imaginative routes to the target. Tickle sometimes, rather than poke.

4. *Robot*. Make your voice and walk robotic as you talk to your partner while walking around the room.

5. *Chin Chuck*. Tickle your partner under the chin.

6. *Mask*. Cover your face with a cloth, move to a foot away from your partner's face, and slowly uncover your face.

7. *Walk Like a Penguin*. Lock you knees, hold your hands out stiffly at your sides, and waddle around your partner.

8. *Where's My Partner*. Cover your partner's face with a cloth. Ask "Where's my partner?." If your partner removes the cloth, say "There's my partner!" If your partner doesn't remove the cloth, you remove it slowly, and say the same thing.

9. *Peek a Boo*. Put cloth over your face and musically ask "Wheeeeeere am I?" After a suspenseful pause, remove the cloth and say "Here I am!"

10. *Squeaky*. Talk to your partner in a squeaky, Mickey Mouse-like voice.

PRONUNCIATION KEY

Key Words	IPA
Lee	i
let	ɛ
Pat	æ
pass	a
stir	ɜ
the	ə
who	u
you	ɪu
would	U
obey	o
all	ɔ
honest	ɒ
fathers	ɑ
pay	e
my	ar
go	o
now	aʊ
their	ɛr
car	ɑr
sing	ŋ
thin	θ
this	ð
shoe	ʃ
pleasure	ʒ
which	hw
chin	ʧ
gin	ʤ

SIMPLE COMIC DIALECT GUIDELINES

A. French

   More nasal than English

   i for I: "ship" becomes "sheep"

   a for e: "ate/eight" becomes "at"

   Trill r

   No h sound

   s for θ: "teeth" becomes "tees"

   z for ð: "this" becomes "zees"

   ʃ for ʧ: "church" becomes "shursh"

   Altered stress: accoun<u>ta</u>ble; <u>a</u>bout; for<u>tu</u>nately; nev<u>er</u>; spite<u>ful</u>; dis-
      <u>a</u>ppear

B. English

   1. Upper Class:

      ɑ for a: "ask" becomes "osk"

      ɔ for a: "all" becomes "oull"

      I for i : "ability" becomes "abiliti"

      ju for u : "duke" becomes "dyuke"

      r: dropped before consonant: "observe" becomes "obseve"

      final r not sounded: "car" becomes "ca"

   2. Lower Class

      I for i : "me" becomes "mi"

      aʊ for u : "too" becomes "tow"

      aI for e: "rain" becomes "ryen"

      no h

      n for ŋ: "walking" becomes "walkin"

      f for θ: "think" becomes "fink"

Glottal stop: "little" becomes "li-le"; "bottle" becomes "bo-le"

C. Russian

i for I: "Italy" becomes "EEtaly"

ε for a: "had" becomes "head"; "bank" becomes "benk"

aʊ for ɔ: "caught" becomes "cowt"

Trill r

d for θ: "this" becomes "dis"

t for d : "told" becomes "tolt"

f for v : "movie" becomes "mofie"

Add k to ŋ: "working" becomes "workingk"

No h

v for w and hw: "where" becomes "vere"; "choir" becomes "kvoir"

D. Greek

i for I : "it" becomes "eat"

d for θ: "this" becomes "dis"

ε for ɜr: "her" becomes "hair"

Trill or tap r

Extra hard h

Add k to ŋ: "running" becomes "runningk"

Point final ed: "walked [walkt]" becomes "walk-ed"

Point final b: "bomb [bom]" becomes "bom<u>b</u>"

E. Italian

Interject "a": "wind" becomes "winda"; "midnight" becomes "mi-danight"; "what you want" becomes "whata you want"

Dropping syllables: "pretty" becomes "prit"; "trouble" becomes "troub"; "very beautiful" becomes "ver beautif"

Use of singular over plural: "these girl"; "plenty gift"

Overuse of present tense: "we eat eight o'clock"; "Tony go yesterday"

Pronoun disagreement: ""this dress, she . . . "; "those men, he . . . "

Avoidance of contractions: "he can't" becomes "he no   c a n " ;
"she isn't going" becomes "she no go"

Avoidance of Comparatives and Superlatives: "more fast"; "most
big"

Omit prepositions: "We go Rome"; "you sit table"

i for I: "it" becomes "eat"; "river" becomes "reever"

u for U: "put" becomes "poot"

Trill r

d for θ

No h sound.

z for s

ZIONE for TION

F. Polish

Same as Greek but with

No final b

v for w: "was" becomes "vas"

t for θ: "think" becomes "tink"

G. Chinese

z or d for θ

Only present tense

r becomes l

l becomes r

i for I: "it" becomes "eat"

H. German

"Air" for "er": "earth" becomes "airth," "her" becomes "hair"

Pronounce final e: "machine" or "name"

Pronounce terminal "ed" not just " 'd"

"e" for "ay": "eight" becomes "et"

v for w

f for v

z for s

p for terminal b

t for terminal d

k for terminal g

s for terminal z

ʧ for ʤ: "Jane" becomes "chain," "badge" becomes "batch"

sht for st: "Street" becomes "shtreet"

ʃp for sp: "spill" becomes "shpill"

I. American Spanish:

I for i: ""it" becomes "eat"

Trill r

d for th

s for z

Drop h

ʒ for ʤ in "George" becomes "Georzh"

i for I: "each" becomes "itch"

add eh to beginning of words which start with s: "ehstart" or "ehspeak"

add d to words beginning with j: dyou or dyes

STAGE TERMINOLOGY

above: adv.) upstage of.

arena stage: n.) a stage with the audience seated on all sides.

below: adv.) downstage of.

blocking: n.) the actors' movements, either suggested by the director or developed "organically" through actors' experimentation.

build: v.) to increase actions in amount, rate, or intensity to a climax.

business: n.) invented physical actions, usually involving stage properties.

cheat: v.) to open the body more than necessary.

close: v.) to turn the torso away from the audience.

cover: v.) 1. to hide a mistake made by a technician or an actor; 2. to block from the audience's view.

cross: v.) to move on the stage

cue: n.) a signal for something to happen; v.) to signal for something to happen.

down: adv.) toward the audience.

downstage: n.) the part of the stage nearest the audience.

fake: v.) to pretend

freeze: v.) to stop all movement.

indicate: v.) to show the outward signs of an attitude or emotion.

open: v.) to turn the front of the torso toward the audience.

plane: n.) an imaginary line parallel to the edge of a stage.

proscenium stage: n.) a stage with the audience seated on one side of a "picture frame" opening, known as the proscenium arch.

share: v.) to stand with another actor on the same plane, in an equally open body position.

stage left: n.) when facing the audience, the side of the stage on the actor's left.

stage right: n.) when facing the audience, the side of the stage on the actor's right.

steal: v.) to move across the stage unobtrusively.

up: adv.) away from the audience.

upstage: n.) the part of the stage furthest from the audience; v.) to force another actor to turn away from the audience by placing yourself in an upstage position.

NOTES

1 "I'm Back, I'm Clean, I Love What I'm Doing", in *USA Today*, February 12, 1987, p. 11A.

2 *The Plays of J. M. Barrie*. (New York: Charles Scribner's Sons, 1928), p. 85.

3 Emerson, Ralph Waldo, "The American Scholar," in *Nature, Addresses and Lectures*. (Boston: Houghton, Mifflin and Company, 1900), p. 103.

4 *New York Times Magazine*, November 26, 1978, p. 36.

5 Bly, Robert, *Iron John: A Book About Men*. (New York: Addison-Wesley Publishing Company, 1990), p. 6.

6 Estes, Clarissa Pinkola, *Women Who Run with the Wolves: Myths and Stories of the Wild Woman Archetype*. (New York: Ballentine Books, 1992), p. 4.

7 Among Terkel's books are *Hard Times, American Dreams, The Good War, The Great Divide, Race*, and *Working*. Other good sources include Joan Morrison's *American Mosaic*, Tom Tiede's *American Tapestry*, Joann Lee's *Asian American Experiences in the United States*, John Gwaltney's *The Dissenters*, David Leviatin's *Followers of the Trail*, Marilyn Davis' *Mexican Voices/American Dreams*, Belinda Hurmence's *My Folks Don't Want Me to Talk*, Theda Perdue's *Nations Remembered*, and John Tenhula's *Voices from Southeast Asia*.

8 Nathan, George Jean, "The House of Satan," in *The House of Satan*. (New York: Alfred A. Knopf, 1926), pp. 3-4.

9 Brando, Marlon, *Songs My Mother Taught Me*. (New York: Random House, 1994), p. 416.

10 Bauer, Susan, *Confiding: A Psychotherapist and her Patients' Search for Stories to Live By*. (New York: Harper Collins Publishers, Inc., 1994), p. 304.

11 Bentley, Eric, *The Life of the Drama*. (New York: Atheneum, 1964), p. 76.

12 *The Autobiography of Malcolm X*. (New York: Grove Press, 1966), p. 172.

13 Schiff, Stephen, "Playing the Diva," in *The New Yorker*, November 14, 1994, p. 112.

14 Jennie Matz.

15 Funke, Lewis and Booth, John E. (Eds.), *Actors Talk About Acting*. (New York: Random House, 1961), p. 17. 16 Thompson, Virgil, "Music Does Not Flow," in *The New York Review of Books*, December 17, 1981, p. 49.

17 Duncan, Ronald, *Collected Plays*. (New York: Theater Arts Books, 1970), p. ix.

18 Wright, p. 285.

19 Wright, p. 285.

20 McAuley, James, *Versification: A Short Introduction*. (Detroit: Michigan State University Press, 1966), p. 23.

21 Joseph, Bertram, *Acting Shakespeare*. (New York: Theatre Arts Books, 1960), p. 22.

22 Joseph, p. 39.

23 Joseph, p. 44.

24 Burton, Hal (ed.), *Great Acting*. (New York: Bonanza Books, 1967), p. 130.

25 Hayworth, D., "The Social Origin and Function of Laughter," in *Psychological Review*, 35, (1928), pp. 367–84.

26 Vygotsky, L.S., *Thought and Language*. Edited by E. Haugmann and G. Vakar. (Cambridge, MA: M.I.T. Press, 1962).

27 Staveacre, T., *Slapstick*. (Sidney: Angus and Robertson, 1978).

28 Haig, Robin, *The Anatomy of Humor: Biophysical and Therapeutic Perspectives*. (Springfield, Illinois: Charles C. Thomas, Publisher, 1988), pp. 105–6.

29 Cooper, Lane, *An Aristotelian Theory of Comedy*. (New York: Harcourt Brace and Company, 1922), p. 61.

30 Schopenhauer, *The World as Will and Idea*. Volume I, p. 76.

31 Kahn, Samuel, *Why and How We Laugh*. (New York: Philosophical Library, 1975), p. 24.

32 Keaton, Buster, *My Wonderful World of Slapstick*. (New York: DaCapo Press, 1982), p. 13.

33 Lahr, John, *Astonish Me*. (New York: The Viking Press, 1973), p. 231.

34 Wilde, p. 166.

35 Wilde, p. 253.

36 Hagen, Uta, *Respect for Acting*. (New York: Macmillan, 1973), p. 166.

37 Cooper, p. 202.

38 Calvert, Louis, *The Problems of the Actor*. (New York: Henry Holt, 1918), p. 152.

39 Ludovici, Anthony, *The Secret of Laughter*. (London: Constable and Company, Ltd., 1932), p. 62.

40 Gythrie, Tyron, *On Acting*. (New York: Viking Press, 1971), p. 12.

41 Kalter, Joanmarie, *Actors on Acting: Preforming in Theatre and Film Today*. (New York: Sterling Publishing Co., 1979), p. 87.

42 Wilde, p. 59.

43 Lahr, John, *American Vaudeville*. (New York: Alfred Knopf, 1984), p. 57.

44 Keaton, p. 207.

45 Cooper, p. 203.

[46] Vaughn, Stuart, *Directing Plays*. (New York: Longman, 1993), p. 258.

[47] David Stern's pamphlets and tapes, *Acting with an Accent*, are available in most libraries. In addition, Appendix 7 provides guidelines for a few stereotypical comic ethnic accents.

[48] Orben, p. 59.

[49] Grotjahn, Martin, *Beyond Laughter*. (New York: McGraw Hill, 1957), p. 261.

[50] Kelly, Emmett, *Clown*. (New York: Prentice Hall, 1954), p. 261.

[51] Keaton, p. 112.

[52] Orben, Robert, *Comedy Technique*. (Hackensack, New Jersey: Wehman Press, 1951), p. 45.

[53] Wilde, Larry, *The Great Comedians Talk About Comedy*. (New York: The Citadel Press, 1968), p. 11.

[54] Wilde, p. 68.

[55] Dance, Daryl Cumber, *Shuckin' and Jivin': Folklore from Contemporary Black Americans*. (Bloomington, Indiana: Indiana University Press, 1978), p. 311.

[56] Vaughn, pp. 253–4.

[57] Orben, p. 48.

[58] Grumet, Gerald W., "Laughter: Nature's Epileptoid Catharsis," in *Psychological Reports*, 1989, V. 65, pp. 1059–78.

[59] Orben, p. 47.

[60] Orben, p. 48.

[61] Orben, p. 45.

[62] Stoufe, L. Alan and Jane Piccard Wunsch, "The Development of Laughter in the First Year of Life," in *Child Development* 43 (1972). pp. 1326–44.

The Real Life of Laurence Olivier

"A PASSIONATE AND MONUMENTAL CELEBRATION OF A GENIUS."
— ARTHUR MILLER,
Front Page, *London Sunday Times*

ROGER LEWIS

"This book confirms Lewis as the most ferociously attentive describer of stage and screen acting since Ken Tynan. It's MAGNIFICENT." — *NEW STATESMAN*

"Forget the standard show business 'life.' Lewis has reinvigorated [the] genre. This is the biography of the year! UNMISSABLE." — *CITY LIFE*

"Dammit, this book is very, very, seductive!" — *KALEIDOSCOPE*

" . . . A MARVELLOUS WORK . . . YOU WILL BE CAPTURED AND CAPTIVATED . . . A MASTERPIECE. DO READ IT." — *THE WESTMINSTER REVIEW*

"Lewis delivers ONE OF THE BEST BOOKS YET ON THE FINE OLD CRAFT OF ACTING." — PATRICK HUMPHRIES, *EMPIRE*

CLOTH • ISBN: 1-55783-298-6

APPLAUSE

SPEAK WITH
DISTINCTION
by Edith Skinner

"Speak With Distinction is the **most comprehensive and accessible speech book available** for teachers and students of speech."
—Joan Washington, RSC, Royal Court
& Royal National Theatre

"Edith Skinner's book is the **best book on speech I have ever encountered**. It was my primer in school and it is my reference book now. To the classical actor, or for that matter any actor who wishes to be understood, this method is a sure guide."
—Kevin Kline

"Speak with Distinction is **the single most important work on the actor's craft** of stage speech. Edith Skinner's work must be an indispensable source book for all who aspire to act."
—Earle Gister, Yale School of Drama

paper•ISBN 1-155783-047-9

APPLAUSE

MONOLOGUE WORKSHOP

From Search to Discovery
in Audition and Performance

by Jack Poggi

To those for whom the monologue has always been synonymous with terror, *The Monologue Workshop* will prove an indispensable ally. Jack Poggi's new book answers the long-felt need among actors for top-notch guidance in finding, rehearsing and performing monologues. For those who find themselves groping for speech just hours before their "big break," this book is their guide to salvation.

The Monologue Workshop supplies the tools to discover new pieces before they become over-familiar, excavate older material that has been neglected, and adapt material from non-dramatic sources (novels, short stories, letters, diaries, autobiographies, even newspaper columns). There are also chapters on writing original monologues and creating solo performances in the style of Lily Tomlin and Eric Bogosian.

Besides the wealth of practical advice he offers, Poggi transforms the monologue experience from a terrifying ordeal into an exhilarating opportunity. Jack Poggi, as many working actors will attest, is the actor's partner in a process they had always thought was without one.

paper•ISBN 1-55783-031-2 • $12.95

APPLAUSE

STANISLAVSKI REVEALED
by Sonia Moore

Other than Stanislavski's own published work, the most widely read interpretation of his techniques remains Sonia Moore's pioneering study, The Stanislavski System. Sonia Moore is on the frontier again now as she reveals the subtle tissue of ideas behind what Stanislavski regarded as his "major breakthrough," the Method of Physical Actions. Moore has devoted the last decade in her world-famous studio to an investigation of Stanislavski's final technique. The result is the first detailed discussion of Moore's own theory of psychophysical unity which she has based on her intensive practical meditation on Stanislavski's consummate conclusions about acting.

Demolishing the popular notion that his methods depend on private—self-centered—expression, Moore now reveals Stanislavski as the advocate of deliberate, controlled, conscious technique—internal and external at the same time—a technique that makes tremendous demands on actors but that rewards them with the priceless gift of creative life.

paper • ISBN: 1-55783-103-3

APPLAUSE

THE APPLAUSE
SHAKESPEARE LIBRARY
General Editor: John Russell Brown

"The Applause Shakespeare is a pioneering edition, responding to an old challenge in a new way and trying to break down barriers to understanding that have proved very obstinate for a long time."
— John Russell Brown

These new Applause editions allow the reader to look beyond the scholarly text to the more collaborative and malleable *performance* text — each note, each gloss, each commentary reflects the stage life of the play.

Available Now:

Macbeth
$7.95 • PAPER • ISBN 1-55783-180-7

A Midsummer Night's Dream
$7.95 • PAPER • ISBN 1-55783-181-5

King Lear
$7.95 • PAPER • ISBN 1-55783-179-3

The Tempest
$7.95 • PAPER • ISBN 1-55783-182-3

Julius Caesar
$7.95 • PAPER • ISBN 1-55783-183-1

❦APPLAUSE❧

SOLILOQUY!

The Shakespeare Monologues
Edited by Michael Earley and Philippa Keil

At last, over 175 of Shakespeare's finest and most
performable monologues taken from all 37 plays are
here in two easy-to-use volumes (MEN and WOMEN).
Selections travel the entire spectrum of the great
dramatist's vision, from comedies and romances to
tragedies, pathos and histories.

*"Soliloquy is an excellent and comprehensive collec-
tion of Shakespeare's speeches. Not only are the monologues wide-ranging and varied, but they are superbly
annotated. Each volume is prefaced by an informative and
reassuring introduction, which explains the signals and
signposts by which Shakespeare helps an actor on his jour-
ney through the text. It includes a very good explanation of
blank verse, with excellent examples of irregularities which
are specifically related to character and acting intentions.
These two books are a must for any actor in search of a
'classical' audition piece."*

ELIZABETH SMITH
Head of Voice & Speech
The Juilliard School

paper•MEN: ISBN 0-936839-78-3
WOMEN: ISBN 0936839-79-1

❦APPLAUSE❦

An Actor and His Time

JOHN GIELGUD

"FUNNY, TOUCHING, BRILLIANT, SPECIAL, THE BEST — EXACTLY LIKE JOHN GIELGUD."
— LAUREN BACALL

"A WONDERFUL BOOK . . . THE RESULT IS MAGICAL . . . GIELGUD IS THE GREATEST ACTOR OF THIS CENTURY . . . WE HAVE NO BETTER CHRONICLER OF THE THEATRE IN HIS TIME . . . AN ASTUTE OBSERVER, A SLY HUMORIST." — SHERIDAN MORLEY,
THE LITERARY REVIEW

"I CAN HEAR HIS SUPERB VOICE IN EVERY LINE."
— ALEC GUINNESS

"A FASCINATING ACCOUNT OF A LEGENDARY CAREER." — *SUNDAY TELEGRAPH*

"A RARE DELIGHT — FULL OF WIT, THEATRICAL HISTORY, ANECDOTES, AND WISDOM."
— DIANA RIGG

CLOTH • ISBN 1-55783-299-4

APPLAUSE

THE ACTOR AND THE TEXT
by Cicely Berry

As voice director of the Royal Shakespeare Company, Cicely Berry has worked with actors such as Jeremy Irons, Derek Jacobi, Jonathan Pryce, Sinead Cusack and Antony Sher. *The Actor and The Text* brings Ms. Berry's methods of applying vocal production skills within a text to the general public.

While this book focuses primarily on speaking Shakespeare, Ms. Berry also includes the speaking of some modern playwrights, such as Edward Bond.

As Ms. Berry describes her own volume in the introduction:

" ... this book is not simply about making the voice sound more interesting. It is about getting inside the words we use ...It is about making the language organic, so that the words act as a spur to the sound ..."

paper•ISBN 1-155783-138-6

APPLAUSE